Robber of the Cruel Streets

The far-reaching effects of his labours can
never be approximately gauged or estimated.
He robbed the cruel streets of thousands of
victims, the gaols of thousands of felons, the
workhouses of thousands of helpless waifs.
And he did it all – to use his own words
– 'with the Sword of the Spirit'.

Daily Telegraph obituary 11 March 1898

CLIVE LANGMEAD

Foreword by George Verwer

Robber of the Cruel Streets

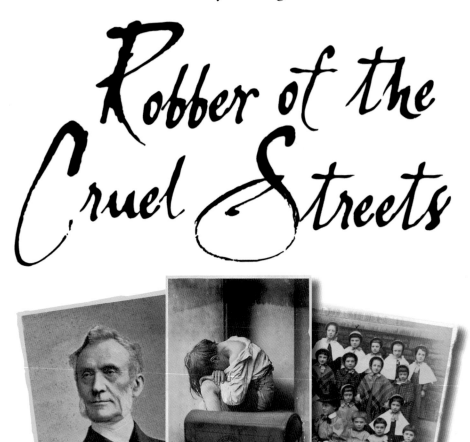

The Prayerful Life of

GEORGE
MULLER

CONTENTS

FOREWORD

George Muller has been a huge influence in the modern mission's movement. As I read this book seven words came to my mind.

Faith – He was a phenomenal example of a faith walk, not just in connection with amazing answers to prayer, but in pressing on through difficulty, disappointment and the fiery darts of Satan.

Love – For me this was the most important reality in his life and was manifested in many different ways. This was worked out in a revolutionary way in the culture of his day. In so many ways, he was a person ahead of his 'day'.

Money – He was very disciplined and careful in the handling of money that came in so many different ways. His reports of how it was used, and his respect for those who gave it is a great example.

Prayer – Reality in love for God and communion with Him just leaps out of the pages in this unique book. We will all have to examine our own lives after reading about it.

Balance – In some areas, like his attitude to reading Christian books, he was extreme, but overall he was a balanced, down-to-earth, practical person. He was, like all of us, learning to integrate the practical and the spiritual.

Vision – I was inspired by his vision for flooding God's Word out around the world. His willingness to travel and preach so much, especially in his senior years, is a fantastic testimony.

Perseverance – People who want to retire and sit back doing little in their senior years will not want to read this book. George Muller was saturated with God's Word and it was demonstrated in his life. To this day thousands of children, and the global Body of Christ, have benefited from this.

To God be the glory.

George Verwer, May 2006

For my wife, Lynette, the music of my life.

INTRODUCTION

George Muller is in your face. That is his problem. Once you know about him, even a very little about him, you start to feel you must avoid the man's gaze. And for good reason. He built orphanages for 2,000 children without asking for a penny. Well, right. The other one's got bells on. But that *is* what he *said* he did. So perhaps he did. £1.3 million income, in Victorian sums, is the conservative estimate, So did he? Really?

That is the first question. It gets worse. Not only did he build and run the orphanages without fundraising of any sort but he further claimed he did so by *prayer*! No clever business plans, tax claw backs or indirect sponsorship schemes. He just prayed. At least, again, that was what he *said* he did. And, it must be confessed, so did a lot of people who worked with him and knew him. Did he delude them *all*? George had grown up at his father's knee and his father was a government tax collector. George certainly knew how to do his books. Or maybe he was just very good at home cooking? His accountants – what did they think? They were as likely to smell a rat as anyone. Surely they could tell if 'creative accounting' was being employed when the annual books were presented. But it seems they concluded much the same as the others. The accounts were watertight.

So was George Muller a remarkable saint and visionary, or charlatan and cheat? If the former, he was pretty impressive and worth listening to, even today; if a cheat, then what did he actually cheat at? And why? He hardly lived an expensive lifestyle. And he did care for 2,050 orphans at a time in five homes, that is undisputed. The buildings he built for them still stand. Perhaps, then, he was a deluded religious fanatic? Victorian institutions were full of such people. Muller was maybe one of the ones they missed. But the City of Bristol came to a standstill for his funeral. Tens of thousands filled the streets. Eighty carriages followed his coffin. Surely he can't have been that deluded?

So this is my attempt to hold his gaze. To learn enough about his life to be able to look him in the eye and say with confidence 'No, all was not what it seemed' or 'Thank you for showing me a more excellent way.'

Clive Langmead
Malvern
April 2006

NOTES:

Those not familiar with Victorian English coinage should note that various terms are used. One pound, or a pound sterling, perhaps two weeks' wages for a labouring man in 1840, was also called a sovereign and was the basic unit of coinage (banknotes did not begin to be printed until 1855). The pound was originally a pound weight of sterling silver, but in Muller's day, as in ours, coins were lighter, effectively money tokens.

A pound (£1) was divided into twenty shillings (20s) and each shilling into twelve pence (12d), then a halfpenny or ha'penny (1/2d), and a quarter of a penny, a farthing (1/4d), which was the smallest coin. A guinea is one pound and one shilling (£1 1s), an old measure to compensate for fraudulent or 'clipped' pound coins.

The pictures in this book that have 'CTA film' in their caption are from film shoots for the accompanying *Robber of the Cruel Streets* film. This is a Christian Television Association drama documentary on the life of George Muller and is available from CWR in both DVD and video formats. More details can be found on the last page of this book.

The actors that appear in this book are as follows: Adam Stone (Muller as a young man); Morgan Philpott (Henry Craik); Rebecca Germain (Mary, Muller's first wife) and Andrew Harrison (Muller as an old man). There are also pictures featuring film extras, the majority of which are from the United Reformed Church in Wrington, Somerset.

CHAPTER ONE

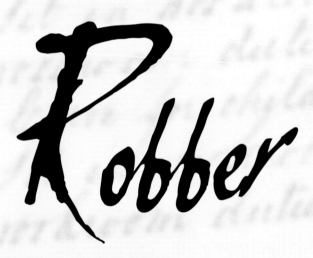

.30. Sit in workroom - till
boys' clothes are ready
the afternoon.

4.30 Walk with boys.

...day:-

10 a.m. Quiet hour.

10.15. Sit in workroom &
workroom duties.

12.30. time for childrens'

4.30 Sit in workroom &
workroom duties. ...

...sday:-

10 Quiet hour.

12.30 Sit in workroom ...

Anyone who has travelled the East Midlands of England, to the regions say of Cambridge or Peterborough, will have a good idea of the countryside around Kroppenstedt in German Saxony where Johann Georg Ferdinand Muller was born on 27 September 1805 – and the villages of Heimersleben, Halberstadt and Shoenebeck where he grew up. Those who haven't, just to need to think of it as flat.

The Leipsig Plain is a long-limbed, occasionally undulating countryside where the sky falls all the way to the far horizon, unbroken and unobscured by hills or mountains. The feeling of endless space and distance is overwhelming. It is like being out on the open ocean, with the land far behind and only a low swell on the sea surface. Except of course that the 'sea' is green or cropped yellow in this, the bread basket of Germany, and from time to time a line of trees, precisely planted, indicates a road striking arrow-straight, across a hedgeless heathland.

This, the southern part of the great North German Plain, makes islands out of the small villages and market communities scattered across it, as it rolls two hundred miles north to the Baltic and North Sea coast and perhaps fifty south across Saxony where the rising Hartz mountains halt its progress. From one village you can usually see the next, or at least the linked twin spires and domed steeples of the two or three churches even the smallest village seems to have spawned, peeping over a low rise or set in the shallowest of valleys.

Georg, as he liked to be called (the 'e' was added when he came to England), was born to a loving, even doting, father – he mentions he was favoured over his elder brother, born in 1803, which he thought was bad for both of them, he gaining an inflated opinion of himself and his brother learning to dislike both his father and Georg. His mother, Sophie Eleonore, was possibly prone to sickness which eventually claimed her when Georg was just fourteen. He did not seem close to his mother and scarcely mentions her in his diaries, recalling her passing with little emotion. But his father, Johann Friedrich Muller, features heavily in his early life and memories.

At the time of Georg's birth, Johann was still serving, or had just left service, as a trumpeter in the 4th Squadron of General

MULLER'S
BIRTHPLACE

Major Quitzlow's Regiment of the Imperial Prussian Cavalry. His war record is unknown, but around this time, perhaps aware of his increasing family responsibilities and the dangers of life in uniform, he left the army to join the fast-growing Prussian Civil Service as a Government Revenue Officer. Or more likely, given it was a time of mobilisation and therefore would not have been easy to resign his military duty, he was lightly wounded in either the Battles of Jena or Auerstadt in 1806 in which Napoleon defeated the Prussian army, and in which Quitzlow's regiment took part, thus pushing him into civilian life by virtue of being unfit for further service in the saddle.

But what is certain is that these political events would have made life for Herr Muller senior and his young family highly complicated, not least because the French then proceeded to occupy most of the area where they lived. This meant the former trumpeter (a trumpeter, although a trooper, was usually a man of considerable intelligence and prestige in the days when trumpet calls were the only method of signalling cavalry manoeuvres) was faced with picking up his new job amongst a maelstrom of ancient and modern civil codes, taxation systems and revenue rates. Some of these were required by the French, some by the Prussians and some by the immediate local authorities in Magdeburg who weren't

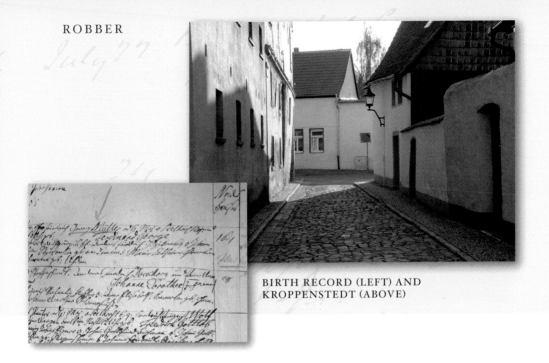

BIRTH RECORD (LEFT) AND
KROPPENSTEDT (ABOVE)

sure which masters they served. But he managed. Perhaps he had learned to keep steady under fire. He was certainly quite tough-skinned, for nobody likes a tax collector and he stuck at it for many years. Either way, slowly but surely, out of this administrative chaos he carved out a new career based on two key things – precise Prussian attention to detail, and money. And in this, with one significant addition, Georg was to prove throughout his life very much his father's son.

As Georg grew, his father consolidated his career. Promotion in 1810 took them from the small house in Kroppenstedt five miles down the road to nearby Heimersleiben, though matters were scarcely more stable in the country as a whole. As little Georg and his brother found their way around their new village they no doubt played at soldiers in the mini fortress there, looking out from its high curtain wall set on the only bluff for miles around, a commanding vista quite new to children growing up on the level plains. But real soldiers were again passing through Saxony. The occupying French, fatally weakened by Napoleon's winter invasion of Russia, were thrown out of Prussia in 1814 and finally defeated, with Prussian intervention, by the Duke of Wellington at Waterloo the following year.

With occupation lifted, the old regime of the now defunct

Holy Roman Empire tried to re-establish itself. But too much had changed. The former rag-tag jigsaw of small states, some church based, some fiercely independent dukedoms, some economic alliances, like the Hanseatic League, and some larger kingdoms like Prussia (which at the time included much of Poland), had been thrown into a melting pot. A pot which would not produce a decent meal until 1871, when Otto Bismarck brought them all together as a new nation called Germany. Until then it would remain an uncertain mess.

So, as Georg grew and showed every aptitude for schooling in both mathematics and classics, father Johann developed a private plan for his life to ensure his son's freedom from the vagaries of war and politics. He would enter him for the Lutheran Church. 'Not,' as Georg recalled, 'so as I might serve God – but that I might have a comfortable living!' And no doubt provide a comfortable

HEIMERSLEIBEN, WHERE MULLER SPENT MOST OF HIS CHILDHOOD

and secure retirement for his father, too, in a minister's expansive country house.

And Georg, at age thirteen or fourteen, was not averse to this. A comfortable living sounded fine to him. And he knew that Lutheran ministers did not actually have to live in a godly way, only appear to do so; and that was something he liked very much. For by then he had proved himself a master of deception. His father had introduced Georg and his brother to money fairly early on in life, giving them quite a sum 'to save' so as, he believed, to help them realise and understand the value of it. 'In order,' commented Georg later, 'to educate us in worldly principles.' But in doing this Johann had opened up a veritable Pandora's Box of worldly principles to his younger son. Georg soon discovered he valued money right enough – but spending it, not saving it.

He had, by age ten, already developed a wide armoury of lies to delude his father whenever he asked to see how Georg's savings were doing – when in fact he had spent most of them. He would falsify his juvenile account book, or double count the money into his hand, or pretend he had left it somewhere else. He later resorted to stealing from his father's revenue receipts left in the house. These losses his father made up himself, thinking he had miscounted, until one day, suspecting his son, he left some money out in a front room. This Georg quickly pocketed or, more accurately, tucked away in a shoe, without a second thought. But the trap was sprung – his father searched him thoroughly and found it.

Georg commented, 'Though I was punished, I don't remember it making any impression on me other than making me think how I might do it more cleverly next time!'

As he grew he did learn to do it more cleverly and, even better, how to use the money he had stolen on more adult pleasures. Pleasures, he candidly admitted later, he indulged in to the hilt. He recalls heavy drinking sessions with school colleagues, playing cards, reading racy novels instead of studying – and modern of moderns – aimlessly strumming his guitar! All this at age fourteen. He hints at darker experiences too – what he later called 'immorality' and 'gross immorality' – a Victorian euphemism for sex, quite probably sex with prostitutes. He certainly had illicit girlfriends – several feature in his early diaries – he chased one he had fallen in love with halfway across the country trying to impress her with extravagant spending.

As his later life shows he learned early the real nature of the cruel streets he'd begun to tread. The inviting firelight glow in the tavern window and the rouge on the cheek of the vamp by the door was most certainly the true colour of desire. But also of danger. And of debauchery – of which he was never proud, even while he indulged it. And of disease, even death. True pleasure was not to be found there, no matter how fiercely he applied himself to run it down. Despite an outward cool reserve he was an intensely passionate man. 'All or nothing' could have been his motto and, as a teenager, he was taking all he could from the world and finding himself increasingly left with next to nothing in the morning. He did not understand why. He only sensed it and privately regretted his personal moral decline. He was later to thank God for His 'infinite patience' but then, he concluded later, he needed more years to drink the cup of self-indulgence completely dry before he was ready to face up to his barrenness of spirit and find a real and worthy object for his passion.

> Despite an outward cool reserve he was an intensely passionate man.

It is significant that the very first orphans the reformed George Muller and his wife opened their doors to in Wilson Street, Bristol, twenty years later, were twenty-six young girls, aged seven to twelve. He knew what happened to young women on the streets. He had no illusions.

But creating illusions became the stock in trade of Georg Muller as he advanced to adulthood. He could fool his loving father much of the time and similarly his friends and acquaintances. He was handsome and feckless, and what he set out to do he did with utter determination and commitment. The trouble was, it was usually illegal.

Deeply offensive, if not illegal, was his honest confession, some years later, that he had gone out playing cards in the early hours the night his mother died, followed by a tavern session and a loud drunken roister about the streets. And all on a Sunday. By then he was living away from home, at least during term time, at Halberstadt Cathedral Classical School in preparation for university. His father came to collect him and his brother the next day for the funeral. To be fair he had not known his mother was dying; but at fourteen, attending a cathedral school, with a view to university and ministry in the Church, to be getting up to such things (especially on a Sunday in a small town), almost beggars belief. His church confirmation service, too, showed that he had a less than godly frame of mind to bring to the ministry for which he was destined. He records he committed 'gross immorality' four days before, and the day before, at formal confession, he gave the clergyman one twelfth of the fee his father had provided for him to be confirmed.

He comments: 'In this state of heart, without prayer, without true repentance, without faith and without knowledge of the true plan of salvation I was confirmed, and took the Lord's supper, on the Sunday after Easter 1820.' The occasion impressed him, at least with its solemnity, and he refused to go out with his friends that day to celebrate. He wanted to think things through. He resolved to turn over a new leaf.

Six weeks later he went to Brunsweig (Brunswick) to stay with his father's sister. He right away formed 'an attachment' to a girl there. And the new leaf began to crinkle. Returning to Halberstadt he kept in touch with her and found he needed to turn over new leaves as fast as he corrupted the old ones. He repeatedly ran out of money and once sank so low as to steal a piece of bread from a soldier billeted in the same house. Worse was to come.

His father was promoted again, moving to the small town of Shoenebeck, nearer to Magdeburg, but retained his house in Heimersleben to put out to rent. Georg immediately requested his father move him from Halberstadt to Magdeburg Cathedral School hoping that a change of school, companions and tutors might somehow improve his degenerate lifestyle. He did not know then that his problems were all his own and would go with him wherever he went. He soon found out. His father brought him to Heimersleben, while the change of school was arranged, to put him in charge of some interior decorating to improve the house for letting. Being his own boss soon went to his head and, stealing some of the building money and more of the revenue money his father had also asked him to collect (but giving, deceitfully, full receipts from the official tax book), he indulged himself all the more, and this culminated in a week of 'pleasure' and 'much sin' in Magdeburg itself. Here he ran through most of his stolen money and allowance. But he was on a roll. Using the last of it he boarded a coach for Brunsweig and the girl, checking into a top hotel on arrival in order to impress her. The money ran out completely after a week, and he was forced to move on.

He went first to his uncle, who took him in, but asked him to leave within a week, no doubt liking the cocksure, hard-drinking teenager no more than one might imagine. Georg then chose a hotel to try and scam in a village nearby. A week on credit saw the manager getting suspicious. Georg swore he would pay, but in the end was forced either to leave his best clothes as security or submit to instant arrest. He left the clothes. Unbelievably he then went out and tried again! Walking to the town of Wolfenbuttle, some six miles away, he signed himself into an inn and began to run up a tab, eating and drinking as though he had a full purse and not a care in the world.

On the third morning, having failed to sneak out of a window (his room being too high up to jump from) he sauntered nonchalantly out of the courtyard hoping to get away. But the alert publican, who had already had his suspicions, spotted him and brought him back. It was time for Georg to bare all. He did, and begged for mercy as a youth, but the innkeeper was unsympathetic and called the town guard. Two soldiers arrested him and took him before the Police Commissioner. He was questioned for three hours and then consigned to Wolfenbuttle Gaol, a grey place of formidable and gloomy aspect established 300 years before, west of the town, in the shadow of Wolfenbuttle Castle. For a boy just sixteen it was not a moment to savour.

OPPOSITE:
OLD PLAN AND
MODERN-DAY
PHOTOS OF
WOLFENBUTTLE
GAOL, WHICH IS
USED AS A PRISON
TO THIS DAY

George Muller's life of prayer

Apart from desperate prayers of the 'Oh God, get me out of this' variety, it is reasonable to assume Muller had few prayers to offer in his wild early years. But one thing of spiritual note comes out of this time, something which came to mean a lot to Muller after he became a Christian, and that is his take on what the apostle Paul called 'election' or 'being one of the elect'.

To a converted Muller, Romans 8:29–30 was a key passage.

> For those God foreknew he also predestined to be conformed to the likeness of his Son, that he might be the firstborn among many brothers. And those he predestined, he also called; those he called, he also justified; those he justified, he also glorified.

To many today the idea that anyone is 'chosen' by God and thus has few options to refuse is rather demeaning. We are taught we are masters of our own fate and even when we become Christians we still carry with us some of this attitude. Surely *we* choose to believe in God? We could easily refuse to do so! And, all in all, quite frankly it is jolly decent of us to believe, given the state of things, pace and pressure of life, tough job, etc. I suspect this how many of us feel, even if it is never voiced.

But with that comes a natural assumption that we will only stay as Christians as long as we hang on for dear life. Hang on to Christ, hang on to faith, hang on to the Bible, to prayer (and that round the clock) and to church. If we don't work at it 24/7 we will very soon lose the plot and slide back into the dark and gloomy mire from whence we came.

But the later Christian Muller did not hold to that. Rather he came to believe that God had set His sights on him from very early on and had then spent a lot of time and trouble getting hold of him. In fact he held that God knew him well before he was born. He noted in both the books of Isaiah and Jeremiah:

'Before I was born the LORD called me;
    from my birth he has made mention of my name.'
(Isaiah 49:1b)

'Before I formed you in the womb I knew you,
    before you were born I set you apart ...'
(Jeremiah 1:5)

Muller's own conversion (see Chapter 3) was, he said, a response to a realisation of the love of God. And whilst realising God could only woo with love, not demand, he believed that God was well capable of engineering circumstances to make that love very apparent and chance after chance would be given to respond to it. Muller does not go as far as saying God dictates who will believe, rather that God, being outside time, knows who will respond and in a sense 'makes' that His will. Muller acknowledges that this is hard to grasp, but this 'elect' viewpoint is perhaps best seen as God reaching down as much, or more, than a believer has to reach up. The good Samaritan stops to help a victim on the road, a father rushes out to meet his prodigal son, a shepherd searches for the lost sheep.

Muller never engaged in any 'long search for God'. He was (he certainly thought) having far too good a time. And anyway he knew all about religion. God had needed to come and get him. And it was a lifetime comfort to Muller to know this. He echoed the psalmist:

Where can I go from your Spirit?
    Where can I flee from your presence?
If I go up to the heavens, you are there;
    if I make my bed in the depths, you are there.
If I rise on the wings of the dawn,
    if I settle on the far side of the sea,
even there your hand will guide me,
    your right hand will hold me fast.
(Psalm 139:7–10)

Muller acknowledged that he had been watched over and cared

for by God as a rebellious youth. He just hadn't known it.

One of the most delightful comments he makes in this context is about his attitude to temptation, which he frankly confesses to facing all his life. He comments: '... should I therefore sin? I should only bring misery into my soul ... for, being a Son of God forever, I should have to be brought back again, though it may be by way of severe chastisement!'

In other words, if he chose to go off the rails, God would be bound to give him an extra hard time in order to bring him back. So it just wasn't worth it!

For our own prayer life

- Being a Christian, life is not just down to us. God is on our side, not standing by watching for us to fail. Grace – God reaching down to help, no strings attached – is a keynote of the Christian faith. No other religion or life system has this key understanding. He cares – above all God cares and is capable of holding onto us even in the toughest times. Our own feelings are a very poor indicator of this loving concern.

- A prayerful reading of the Bible passages Muller favoured concerning God's special interest in and devotion to each one of us is a very powerful way of gaining personal confidence.

- God takes risks, forging (and forgiving) from the most unpromising stock. That includes us. Our job is to pray for those we care about and those we feel burdened for. Some of the 'toughest' have met God and changed. Remember Paul the apostle.

CHAPTER TWO

Captive

30. Set in workroom. See
boys' clothes are ready
the afternoon.

4.30 Walk with boys.

——————

…sday:—
10 a.m. Quiet hour.
12.15. Set in workroom a…
workroom duties.
care for children's …
12.30. Set in workroom a…
4.30 workroom duties. S…

——————

…sday:—
11 Quiet hour.
12.30 Set in workroom.
…

Now secured in one of the most notorious jails of the region, as he put it, 'along with convicted thieves and murderers', Georg woke the next morning a very sad, and, in his own estimation, 'most wretched' boy. His 'superior manners' as he called them had attracted slightly better than average prison fare the night before. Meat with the bread and water. No doubt the warders were hoping for some small change in return for favourable service to the new prisoner. But they were out of luck. Georg had nothing and was arrogant to boot. Treatment reverted to prison standard. In fact on that first evening he had not even touched the better food. After four days he was desperate even for the bread and water.

He commented, 'Here I was; no creature with me; no book, no work in my hands and large iron rails before my narrow window, locked up in this place day and night.' Self-pity, yes. Remorse, no.

He asked for a Bible, simply, he says, for something to read, and possibly in a feeble attempt to create a good impression. It was refused. He then asked for the inmate of the next cell, a thief whom he had spoken to briefly by shouts, to be put in with him – for company. This was granted. But within days they had fallen out, Georg having spun ridiculous tales of wild adventures in order to impress the man. After a while his cell mate refused to talk to him. So they sat there, day after day, ignoring each other. Christmas 1821 came and went and no one visited. He heard from no one. Despair was setting in when on 12 January he was called into the Police Commissioner's office. The news was good. The Commissioner had contacted Georg's uncle in Brunsweig who had in turn written to his father. He had just sent money to pay off the hotel and the inn, the prison maintenance fees and a coach fare home. No one was pressing charges, so Georg was free to go.

As the massive wooden gates of the prison swung closed behind him some might suppose that this short sharp shock and the prospect of his father's wrath, or even disappointment, might have had some impact on Georg's outlook. Not in the least. First he deliberately neglected to call on the sister of his former cell mate, something he had promised faithfully he would do, then he chose to laugh and leer his way home to Heimersleben with the worst travelling companion he could find on the stage.

His father soon arrived, beat him severely and took him back to Shoenebeck, determined to keep him on a tight rein from now on. But Georg was irrepressible. Nevertheless, knowing that his father's favour was what mattered, if not personally then at least for the signing of parental documents, passports, provision of college fees and so on, he kept his head down, at least in appearance. And he sought to reclaim lost ground by doing the only thing he knew would impress his father – making money. He took in private pupils, teaching them Latin, French, German grammar and arithmetic among other things. Georg was certainly no dunce. As well as this he was progressing his own studies towards entering a pre-university school the 'Gymnasium' – the great hope his father still held out for him. Earning well and presenting a courteous rather than arrogant side to everyone, he was soon bringing in more than enough to cover his living costs and became well liked in Shoenebeck. And became 'no expense to my father and earned more than I cost him'. Johann was delighted. Prison had obviously been a turning point. A moment of truth in his son's life. A valuable, if regrettable, lesson.

'But,' recalls Muller, 'all this time I was in my heart as bad as ever; for I was still in secret habitually guilty of great sins.' The leopard was evidently quite incapable of changing his spots.

Georg's real nature surfaced when the time came to go on to the Gymnasium. Halle Gymnasium had a reputation for strictness. Added to that, a number of Georg's older friends would be at the university – as undergraduates – but Georg would still be at the Gymnasium as a schoolboy and treated as such. Not good for his pride. Also, from a certain coyness at this point in his diary, it is likely there was yet another girl to be reckoned with. And she didn't live in Halle. So, while pretending to his father he was setting off for the entrance exam in Halle, he took the stagecoach in the other direction into the Hartz mountains and the town of Nordhausen! There the Gymnasium director, somewhat surprised, examined him, was duly impressed and, liking him, offered him a place on the spot. Georg returned home, saying nothing except that he had been accepted for Gymnasium education.

The next few weeks stretched Georg's imagination to the limit as story on story had to be concocted to cover his errant tracks. He talked about the interesting journey to Halle, the splendid Gymnasium buildings, the kind director and tutors and the delightful setting of the famous Lutheran University itself on the banks of the River Saale. Incredibly, he managed to hold it all together until the day before his departure. Then, with one slip his 'whole chain of lies' snapped and the secret came out. His father went off like one of the French cannons he'd been trained to capture and Georg was made to feel that being locked up in Wolfenbuttle Gaol might be a softer option.

But tears and entreaties, allied to the solid fact that Georg's abilities had been recognised, eventually won the day. Georg was sent to Nordhausen for two and a half years. There he became to all intents not only an exemplary student, but an exceptional one. He could talk fluently in Latin, which he routinely did on walks with the Gymnasium director, who then proceeded to point Georg out to the others as his most impressive pupil. Which he certainly was. He routinely studied from 4am to 10pm, reading exhaustively of the writings of Voltaire and Moliere, the most highly-regarded French philosophers of the day, as well as many classical thinkers including Horace and Cicero. He possessed over three hundred books, 'but no Bible' he comments dryly, later. This excepted – something he naturally came to regard later as an appalling omission – his pre-undergraduate school work was thorough, studious and ably completed. He was a model student.

There was only one small, but indicative, crack in his facade: having again run up several significant debts he decided to solve the problem by engineering a robbery. First he showed his father's monthly allowance round the school when it was sent to him then, later, breaking the lock on his guitar case and trunk, he rushed to the director's office in disarray, with his coat flung off, exclaiming the money had been stolen. His shocked friends immediately took up a collection to replace it. He now had double the money to pay off his debts! And those he still owed also gave him longer to pay, hearing of the robbery.

> He possessed over three hundred books, 'but no Bible' he comments dryly, later.

But despite outward support the director had a vague sense that all was not what it seemed. He did not call in the police, for which Georg, with his criminal record, was supremely grateful, noting that they would quickly have found the real culprit – but the walks to talk Latin quietly stopped. All in all Georg was pleased shortly to be moving on from Nordhausen.

In the spring of 1825 the Martin Luther University in Halle, near Leipzig, was a most august theological establishment, founded in 1694 as the primary Lutheran, and therefore Protestant, university in a continental Europe deeply divided along confessional lines. It had also just combined, in 1817, with Wittenburg University, which was where Luther had first made his 'protest against indulgences' in 1517 by hammering his theses onto the church door. In Halle the study of formal Lutheran theology was serious business. That is not to say that in German-speaking central Europe, Protestants and Catholics had not learned to live and work together side by side. In many communities, in what was still a 70 per cent rural church-based culture, they often did, remarkably more so than in many other countries at the time, though Austria and Poland remained almost wholly Catholic. But the growing Prussian political influence meant that an uneasy balance had had to be struck between the two religious viewpoint's political lobbies.

HALLE UNIVERSITY
TODAY

Educationally Halle represented the spearhead of Protestant thinkers, politicians and churchmen, as did Bonn for the Catholic. So at Halle Lutherans aimed high. There, when Georg arrived, of 1,260 students 900 studied divinity. But to even the most sincere, the idea that actual belief might be involved was faintly ridiculous. As Georg wryly observed later, 'of all the nine hundred probably not nine genuinely feared the Lord.'

Georg was delighted to be there. The cheerful, bustling narrow streets, the groups of bright young students with whom to laugh and joke, the chance for shady walks down by the river bank by the Giebichenstein Roman fortress, the town spread out behind, seemingly looking up in awe and respect at the university buildings perched impressively on the brow of the hill.

The campus was a short step up from the mediaeval market square with its large church and imposing clock tower and, more important to Georg, its abundance of welcoming half-timbered taverns. But it was below the town, in a curve of the river, where Georg went to live as a new student for his first two months. Somewhere that would have an

HALLE MARKET SQUARE CHURCH (LEFT) AND DR AUGUST HERMANN FRANCKE (ABOVE)

extraordinary influence on his later life: the Francke Foundation. Student hostel, orphanage, school house and workshop complex. It was, and is, an impressive, even massive collection of buildings, founded in 1698 by one Dr August Hermann Francke, professor of Greek and Hebrew at the very new Halle University. And even when Muller arrived it was already, as it is now, a major tourist feature of the town.

It was a model of self-contained charity from a previous century. Rather like Father Flanagan's 'Boys' Town' in 1930s Nebraska, the Foundation had been set up in a poor Halle suburb, Glaucha, by an energetic, public-spirited and overtly Christian man. Dr Francke had created a mix of schools for parented as well as orphaned children, orphan accommodation, a library, trade workshops, a printing press, bookshops, paper mill, pharmacy, gardens and a dairy. He was no Lutheran formalist. In fact they hated him, having had him thrown out of Leipzig for changing the theology syllabus to a more faith-centred one. But he loved his God intimately, and it showed in a life of intense faith, love and social activity on behalf of others; especially children. Especially orphans. He called himself a pietist. This very simple Christian viewpoint, so called because it was first developed by 'pious' groups in Frankfurt, was for a real, devoted, Bible-centred, personal religion. In fact if it wasn't real, devoted and personal you could leave out the religion. But never the Bible.

When Georg stayed there before obtaining more convenient digs nearer the Divinity Faculty he could not have cared less about any of this. But something in him took note. Later he was to remember Dr Francke and his orphanage. And that memory would come to have more influence for the direction and shape of his life than almost anything else.

Now into Muller's life enters the more direct and apparent hand of God. In the shape of a rather miserable student, who had turned his back on his faith and was looking for a good time in bad company – and at the time you couldn't get much better bad company than Georg Muller. Christoph Friedrich Beta, who had known Georg in Nordhausen, was sitting in a student tavern one day when Georg walked in. Georg was in a rather odd frame of mind. He had just found out that only 'decent' divinity students got decent Lutheran parishes. If word got back to the Divinity Faculty that you 'enjoyed life' too much as a student, or at least could not be discrete about it, well, you still got a job on graduation, but life among the herring fishers of the East Fresian Islands or a mission among the salt miners of Krakow was not what Georg, or his father, quite had in mind.

So Georg was on the look out for calmer company. And in Christoph he thought he had found just the man. He knew him as a quiet, uninspiring lad, rather religious (he came from a pietist family) which was the tone he felt it ideal to adopt if he was going to improve his chances of finding a safe, comfortable Lutheran parish. To be fair, too, he was having pangs of conscience. He wanted to be good. To be a good church minister. He was actually enjoying high living less and less. But all his noble resolutions still ended speedily enough at the prospect of another foaming tankard or wild night out on the town – still paid for, it seems, by pawning his watch, his linen and much of his good clothing.

He had also developed a passion for travel. In July 1825 he, Christoph and two other students, rented a post-chaise and toured the countryside for four days. Not a cheap undertaking, paid for by pawning more clothing. Excited by this, Georg then chose to challenge his friends to mount an expedition to Switzerland! Sweeping aside all his companions' minor objections – no money, no passports, no parental permission, no maps or guides, Georg cooked up a typically devious Muller solution. He carefully forged letters of permission from the relevant parents and used these to get passports, issued in Halle. He then ran through his own, Christoph's and his companions' divinity study books and set aside a number which he took to the pawnbrokers. Hey presto! Travelling expenses. As for guides, well, they would have to trust to luck. Georg later commented that he believed God was especially looking out for them on this particular journey so many were the narrow scrapes they got into.

They set off on 18 August and spent forty-three days on the road, most of it on foot. They travelled as far south as Mount Rigi which both dominates and provides the beautiful dramatic skyline around Lake Lucerne. Mount Rigi was then, and is now, the most popular mountain to climb in the country (mainly today because you can take a train right to the top). Georg's party had to climb on foot but he marvelled at the staggering view. After this he felt he could say, with the ancient Roman poet Horace, '*Vixi*! – Now I have lived!' But it was, inevitably with Georg, at the expense of the others. On the trip he had made sure he was controller of the funds – and fixed it so that he paid around a third less than the others for everything. They never knew.

He noted: 'I had now obtained the desire of my heart. I had seen Switzerland. But I was far from being happy.'

Returning home he had to invent a web of lies to convince his father he had been travelling relatively cheaply and much more locally. Switzerland would have seemed like the North Pole to his father. And expensive. But this time the dam of deceit held. His father was convinced. But Georg's conscience pricked. He resolved, having 'lived', he would, he really would, reform.

On his return for the next term he noted: 'I was different for a few days; but when the vacation was over, and fresh students came, and, with them, fresh money, all was soon forgotten.' It was evident that no power on earth could reform Georg Muller, least of all he himself.

But he didn't know that by now the 'Hound of Heaven'[1] was in hot pursuit. And closing fast.

1. *The Hound of Heaven*, a poem on God's outreaching love by Francis Thompson (1893).

George Muller's life of prayer

Though still not praying in any informed way himself at this time, Muller acknowledged later that circumstances in his life in Halle conspired to draw him towards God. Key to this was the friendship with Christoph Beta. Only in retrospect could he see the jigsaw pieces clicking into place.

It seems the first active player on the spiritual field was not actually Christoph but his father. Muller recorded later that Christoph came from a Christian, most probably 'pietist', household where the Bible was read, believed and treasured rather than just opened formally in church which was what Muller was used to. Christoph had grown up with prayers being offered from the heart, spontaneously, not just intoned. There was real faith in his home.

Muller later explained the sequence of events, tied in with the Beta family, which led to the impact on his own soul.

It seemed that Christoph had not taken to the carefree life of a backpacker in Switzerland as much as he had expected – or pretended. Whilst superficially seeming to have a good time, he had begun to feel the journey was, to put it mildly, inappropriate. Funding it by pawning the books his father had bought for study certainly was, so was the company they kept and the scrapes they got into. Christoph had begun to feel pretty guilty about it all. And there was pressure on his spirit too. Perhaps because his believing parents were praying for him at the time, as they probably did whenever he was away from home. Perhaps they had also noticed, from the tone of his letters and visits home, a cooling of his faith since he had gone to college. A time of concern for every faithful parent, now as then. As for being away for the summer they probably thought he was just touring locally or had been detained by extra study at Halle. They, like Georg's father, would have been very surprised to know their Christoph had gone roaming as far as Switzerland.

The deception bothered Christoph a lot more than it did Georg. Christoph already knew morals were not a matter of convention, to be misused by smart people like Georg, but a measure of true stature and of integrity.

So, shortly after the Swiss trip, Christoph broke down in front of his father and confessed all. The large-hearted man, having no doubt made some sharp points about honesty, forgave him and sent him back to Halle, shouldering, one can imagine, an even greater burden to pray for his son. And probably to pray for the errant head of the Swiss adventure, his son's friend Georg.

But he did not only pray. He acted. Christoph was put in touch with a Dr Richter, who in turn gave him a letter of introduction to a man on the spot in Halle. A believing Christian, also probably a pietist, Johann Wagner of No 7, Kleine Steinstrasse, living just three streets away from the university campus. There Christoph could find a stabilising home-from-home and supportive believers. No doubt Herr Wagner was contacted separately and told to look out for young Christoph. And he in his turn may well have left a note at the student's digs to say 'drop by any time'. If not, Christoph Beta was certainly told that on his first visit, as was Muller on his. But that is running ahead in the story.

What is also very likely is that the little group which met weekly to pray and read the Bible at Kleine Steinstrasse started praying for both Christoph and Georg. They had been asked by a worried father to support these young people, and they fully intended to.

All his life Muller commented on the value of this kind of personal prayer for individuals. Quite apart from a life of praying for all sorts – orphanage funds, church and administrative problems, health problems and so on, he took it upon himself to pray for certain individuals to become Christians. He did not pray for every non-Christian he met, only those whom he felt God had 'laid on his heart'. Those for whom he sensed God was giving him a burden in his spirit to pray for. Then he did not let go!

Towards the end of his life he recalled in his diary five in particular.

> In November 1844, I began to pray for the conversion of five individuals. I prayed every day without a single intermission, whether sick or in health, on land or sea, whatever the pressure of my engagements.

After twelve years three of the five had become Christians. After fifty years one more. Muller thanked God and went on praying. By his death in 1898, fifty-four years after he had first felt called to pray for the five, the remaining one still had not made any commitment, though prayed for by Muller to the end. It was reported he became a Christian early the next century!

For our own prayer life

- Christian prayer reaches the parts others cannot reach. It passes through space and time and, drawing on massive resources, can touch and support even those who wilfully reject sound help and advice. But it is not self-actuating. We must set time aside to do it. There is no way round this.

- We must be prepared to *act* in a godly way as well as pray, though prayer should come first (not second) to enhance and confirm the action. As the British writer Edmund Burke (1729–1797) said, 'all that is necessary for the triumph of evil is that good men do nothing'. And women.

- Prayer should be specific. This includes prayers of thanks and praise. General prayers are of low value, showing little care and less thought. In style these are similar to 'personalised' marketing mail shots – and about as effective. But focused prayer somehow releases the Holy Spirit to work remarkably energetically. There is no limit to the good directly applied prayer can achieve. In effect, Christoph's father was the man behind all the Muller homes and Georg's life's work!

CHAPTER THREE

Freeman

30. Sit in workroom. last
boys' clothes are ready...
the afternoon.

4.30 Walk with boys.

10 a.m. Quiet hour.
10.15. Sit in workroom and
workroom duties.
10.30. ...se for children's
4.30 Sit in workroom and
workroom duties. ...

10 Quiet hour.
10.30 Sit in workroom. ...
duties

The pivotal moment of Georg's life crept up on him unawares. His drinking crony Christoph Beta fresh back in university, chastened by his honest dealings with his father and in weekly contact with Johann Wagner, boldly asked Georg while on a walk if he would like, as a divinity student, to try something different from the usual run of taverns and worse. How about a prayer meeting? This was an offer nervously made, as Muller later records, Christoph believed he would be laughed right out of the Marktplatz in between tankards. But it didn't happen. Something intrigued Georg about the invitation. He asked what went on and, on being told it was Bible reading, singing and prayers, something moved him to accept. In fact he was eager to do so.

Next Saturday, a darkening November evening in 1825, saw the two young men slipping down through the narrow lanterned and cobbled streets from the university faculty to No 7 Kleine Steinstrasse and knocking on the door. Herr Wagner was already there as was the little Bible study group. The students were welcomed with words that Muller never forgot. He had automatically made a courteous apology for dropping by unannounced. Johann immediately replied 'Come as often as you please, house and heart are open to you.' Muller was struck by the simple honesty of the invitation. It was not form, it was meant.

The two young men followed Herr Wagner into the parlour and sat down. The meeting opened with a hymn, then one Friedrich Kayser knelt down and informally asked a blessing on the group. Georg was stunned. He had never seen anyone on his knees before and he himself had never prayed on his knees. Herr Kayser then read a chapter of the Bible and followed this with a printed sermon. Prussian law at the time demanded no extempore preaching without an ordained minister present due to the volatile relationships between the political confessional camps. They then sang another hymn and Johann Wagner prayed. It was a rough, unrehearsed prayer, that of a tradesman, which was what he was; but Georg, highly-educated undergraduate, felt, even with all his theological learning, 'I could not pray as well'. He recalls: 'the whole made a deep impression on me.'

Suddenly he realised he was, for the first time, truly happy. A sense of peace entered his soul. But 'if I had been asked why – I could not clearly have explained it'. He walked back to the campus with Christoph on a cloud of pure joy.

'All we have seen on our journey to Switzerland, and all our former pleasures, are as nothing in comparison with this evening,' he enthused. He went to sleep that night, 'peaceful and happy in my bed'.

It was a turning point. 'All my sins were not given up at once,' he affirms. But right away he gave up friends who he knew to be wicked. He stopped going out for evenings in taverns to get drunk and his honesty quotient increased by the day. 'But still a few times after this I spoke an untruth,' he confessed. He owned to being overcome by sin from time to time, but not without 'sorrow of heart' and it was far less frequent. He was now on an upward not downward spiral. He went round to Johann Wagner's the next day, and the next – and twice more that week. He prayed open honest prayers in his own words and read the Bible with increasing and genuine interest. He went to church now 'from the right motives' – and was laughed at roundly by all his fellow students.

But he did not care; something that would become his style for life. If Christ was for it then Muller was into it, no matter how much ridicule was thrown at him, or how much opposition put up. It was to him all very obvious. He often recounted later how 'simple' he found real faith. There were few complexities to him. He had seen that being wholly selfish, even when crafty and well educated, had got him precisely nowhere; neither enlarging his personal wealth nor the wealth of his spirit nor, more important, had he become an acceptable person to himself. He had been living a lie, as well as living as a liar. Now he could live an authentic life. This was real and thrilling. The consequence of being saved from the judgment of a powerful if invisible God was not then understood, or only dimly. He simply knew that pleasing himself was useless. A living death. And now he had been made alive. He felt re-born. Given another chance. Put in touch, miraculously by some grace, with the Author of life itself. It was later, as he studied the Bible more and more with the eyes of faith, that he discovered that re-birth really was what had happened to him and that a rich life in eternity was now his destiny, not the wasteland of hell which it had been; something of which he had already had

NO 7 KLEINE STEINSTRASSE

JOHANN WAGNER

a foretaste even in this life. What did he care what others thought! Compared to the splendour of knowing God, what was a little dismissive laughter? In fact it was probably a good thing to help to puncture his pride.

Georg committed himself passionately to his new life, attending the meetings at Kleine Steinstrasse regularly, and also calling in there between divinity lectures. But if his destiny had changed and his path was now upward, old desires still threatened. There was a spiritual and moral war on and 'the common temptations of Satan', as he put it, were all around. He might have slipped out of Satan's net by a miracle of grace, but throughout his life he would never swim fully free of spiritual entanglement.

> There was a spiritual and moral war and 'the common temptations of Satan', as he put it, were all around.

At Muller's conversion Satan was one very unhappy angel and would become increasingly so as Muller's love of God grew and a calling to serve Him in teaching and preaching hardened. Muller often said that one of the chief tactics Satan used to attempt to defuse his ministry was diversion. Getting him off track, so his considerable energy would be wasted in matters 'not of God's immediate purpose' (though they might well be generally worthy or even apparently godly). So the first battle of a long campaign against Muller's newly devoted soul was launched. And, as so often happens, it came only a matter of weeks after his conversion. To Muller the instrument of diversion was carefully, even cyncially, chosen: a Christian girl at Herr Wagner's prayer meeting.

Georg had gradually become attracted to her at the same time as discovering he felt called to mission work. The spreading of the gospel in other lands seemed to him not only godly pressure on his spirit but something he had been gifted to do with his easy command of languages, theological background (his divinity studies now filled with new meaning) and an ability to communicate ideas authoritatively.

But the girl, who it seems returned his interest, was not to be allowed by her parents to undertake the hazards of missionary service. As he struggled with this, Georg's prayers first lapsed into cold formality then the time lengthened between any prayer at all. His joy evaporated. Weeks went by as he focused on the girl, trying to work out a long-term future with her. Then at Easter time 1826 a young man called Hermann Ball came to Halle. He was a missionary to Polish Jews – a demanding and committed Christian work for a man who came from a wealthy family and who could have easily taken up light work locally with his parents' blessing. Georg was impressed by Hermann's forthright practical and costly faith and felt forced to face his own increasing coolness towards God – and the reason for it, though nothing remotely improper had taken place between himself and the girl. He was shocked to find how far he had neglected his new faith as a consequence – apparently in all innocence. There and then he broke off the attachment and re-dedicated his life to God in fervent prayer. He records that the relationship had not so much been wrong but something that he 'had entered into without prayer'.

The moment he decided on the break he felt he immediately received 'the peace of God that passes all understanding' and bent his will back to the missionary call he believed he had received. He records nothing of what the girl thought about all this, but from Muller's point of view it had been a close call. A dangerous diversion; the good having become the enemy of the best. But afterwards, 'I was for the first time in my life able fully and unreservedly to give myself up to Him'.

Nevertheless Muller's entanglements continued. He candidly confesses to various temptations, when feeling down or out of sorts. He still drank wine and beer from time to time 'in a backsliding state ... drinking merely for the sake of drinking' though nothing like the ten pints of an afternoon he had been used to. His conscience was now informed and invigorated and 'within one or two glasses my conduct was brought before me'. Given that in later years his orphanages were given donations of beer in casks, which he gladly accepted, it does not seem that he ever objected to alcohol per se; just its use for selfish excess. In later Victorian times in Britain the scourge of the 'penny gin shops' in many cities hardened Christian opinion against alcohol in any form and with so many Victorian Christian groups occupied at street level in social concern – from

GEORG MULLER
(CTA FILM)

Booth's Salvation Army to George William's YMCA and Elizabeth Fry's prison reform – prohibition became an important tool in rebuilding broken lives and families. Muller, with his own intimate concern for life on the streets, supported this.

In Halle a mentor for his missionary interest was soon supplied in the shape of one Dr Friedrich Tholuck, Professor of Divinity in Halle and one of the few in the Faculty who genuinely 'feared the Lord'. One of the first things Dr Tholuck did was to introduce Georg to some American academics (one was later to become Dean of Harvard) who desperately wanted to learn German. They paid well for his lessons and this helped Georg get through the rest of his degree. For by this time his father had cut him off. What wasting and whoring, and even prison, could not achieve, conversion had. Shocked by Georg's new-found religious enthusiasm, added to Georg's desire to give up the prospect of a comfortable life of a country parson to become a missionary, his father had also sharply pointed out he had invested much in Georg's education. Now he would get nothing back for it. Then he broke down in tears and said Georg 'was no longer his son'. But Georg stood firm in his sense of calling, during what must have been an emotional and personally confusing interview. Was he honouring his father, as Scripture demanded, by giving up the comfortable prospect his father wanted? Or was there now a higher calling? He felt there was. Muller had begun to transform his headstrong nature into nerves of steel. He would need to. To show good faith he resolved never to ask for any more money from his father. He never did and in fact in later years cleared a number of his father's debts.

Another problem thrown up by his father's refusal to accept his new calling was that no mission would accept him. In Prussia a father's permission was a pre-requisite to join any missionary society. But Georg didn't mind; God would find a way. He was forced to look for cheaper college digs, too, his first move taking him to free rooms for poor students in the Francke Institute. Francke's example was again seen and experienced first hand. It stayed in his mind.

About this time, in August 1826, Muller preached for the first time to help out an elderly clergyman. His approach was typical – of the old Muller. He got hold of a printed sermon, re-wrote it in his own hand and commenced to learn it. It took him a week to learn what was almost an hour's delivery. On the Sunday he delivered it, twice, once at an early service and once at the mid morning. Then he had a problem. In his enthusiasm he had agreed to take the afternoon service too. What to preach? He took his courage in both hands and read out a verse or two from Matthew chapter 5. He looked up and started making comments on the first beatitude 'Blessed are the poor in spirit' and found that he seemed, quite literally, to be inspired. The words came easily and enjoyably. And the congregation seemed interested and involved, which they had not been in the morning. He spoke simply and directly, feeling that this was 'a blessed work'. So lifted was he that after the service he 'left the aged clergyman as soon as possible, lest I should lose my enjoyment!'

His interest in mission increased by the day, fanned by the enthusiasm of Dr Tholuck. He distributed monthly '300 missionary papers' and sold and gave away many tracts, going for walks with his pockets stuffed full of them. He had also started a small Bible meeting on Sunday evenings in his lodgings for fellow believing students (about six, rising to twenty by the time he left Halle). But he was, as expected, refused entry to The Berlin Missionary Society, as his father had refused his consent.

He was wondering how to get round this when he heard that a society in England – The Continental Society – was looking to send a man to Bucharest, where many German speakers lived. Georg offered his services with Dr Tholuck's enthusiastic support and testimonials. We may see the good Doctor's influence, too, in that Georg's father agreed to this service, something Georg hailed, rightly, as a miracle.

At the same time there appeared in Halle his old friend and inspirer Hermann Ball. He was in poor health and wondered how long he could continue to serve the Jews of Poland. Georg was a Hebrew enthusiast – would he consider taking on some of this burden? Georg was torn; but considered God would decide. Within ten days Dr Tholuck told him war had broken out between Turkey and Russia and that they were fighting in Bucharest. The Society had changed its mind. It was too dangerous to send anyone. Rejoicing, Georg fired off a letter to the London Society for Promoting Christianity among the Jews. They sent back some questions and, after inspecting the replies, waited seven months before offering him a probationary six months as a missionary student – if he would come to London. Georg was not amused. It was June 1828, he had finished his degree and life was ahead of him. Go back for more school? To London? Why not Warsaw and get straight into action? Plus they were hardly begging for him. Seven months is a long time to kick your heels – though he had in fact found a temporary job as chaplain to a new criminal workhouse in Halle.

So maybe the Lord had spoken. Maybe not. He was not sure but, after praying much and visiting his father, he decided to go. The pull of learning Hebrew properly for six months was as decisive as anything. But there was one small fly in the ointment. Something he had been putting off for some time. He had to complete one year of military service at his own expense (as he had a degree and was therefore from a professional family), or three at the government's. Unless he could get an exemption from the Kaiser himself. This was quite possible – sympathy for missionary work had led to exemptions in the past. So Georg made use of some Christian contacts in the military. They wrote letters and tried to pull some strings. All came back with the same answer: No. The king of Prussia was beginning to have ambitions to pull together a new country called Germany. France was fast recovering in the West, the Russians stirring to the East (hence the problems in Bucharest) and, though German speaking, Austria was a very tentative ally who might well, and eventually did, become an enemy. Kaiser Frederick Wilhelm III was going to need all the troops he could get. Georg's intended service of a heavenly King would have to wait until he'd served under a temporal. But to Georg, in his new simple and direct way of seeing things, no earthly king could stand in the way of the King of kings. It was all a matter of faith. No, actually, it was a matter of power.

George Muller's life of prayer

Conversion is a great mystery. God's Spirit moves, convicts and saves where He wills. There are things we can look at in people's lives which may seem to lead to them admitting of spiritual poverty, or a need for (God's) love, or a search for a Great Creator, or a sense of failure or guilt which needs sorting out. But in the end, the prayers of others, combined with a personal nakedness of spirit before a loving, but wholly just, Presence achieve a spark of responsive faith which is fanned into flame. How or why we can never really know. It is rightly put beyond us. It is entirely personal and individual to each.

Muller was not preached to, or confronted with his need of a Saviour, nor was he challenged by his sin, or threatened with hell. In a sense it seems his eyes were opened by honesty. Johann Wagner's open invitation to 'visit any time' stood in contrast to the familiar, but meaningless, invitations he was used to. He saw a heartfelt prayer actually spoken from the heart, he noted an honest respect for a difficult law (who would have known if the little group had chosen to listen to their own speaker?). There was also the clear family discipline, but loving restoration, of his friend Christoph set against the indecision of his own father's dealings with him and his brother. And there was the reality of love in the group.

It is evident his prayer relationship with God was immediate and personal from the start. He 'knew' God immediately in some measure. The rest of his life was thereafter a drive to get to know him better. Biblical 'knowing' is very intimate – a common joke of course – but it seems Muller really did know God in almost this highly intimate way. His was not the cold formal prayer life of a Victorian black suit and starched collar. He was a warm man, courageous and (to start with) impulsive. Muller had a passionate relationship with God. God loves passion, often seeming more ready to understand passionate people, even those who powerfully sin (see King David in 2 Samuel 11), though God demands proper repentance. Those who are passionate at least tend to *do* something!

(Remember God's hatred of the 'lukewarm' church of Laodicea in Revelation 3:16.) Muller was a passionate convert and it showed. He prayed because it mattered.

Despite this intimate walk with God he was always aware of the presence of his 'old self' throughout his life. He knew what he had been saved from. Not only eternal damnation but a pretty sordid and superficial lifestyle. He never forgot what he had nearly become. Many who become Christians have never had the courage to sin as deeply as George. Dipping a toe in the pool they giggle a bit and draw back, afraid to go further but always wondering what they've missed. George had plunged in good and proper and could tell everyone that he'd found the water pretty uninviting. He always honestly (that word again) admitted to continual temptation in one direction or another and to his mind this showed the attraction of sin was more than an intrinsic offer of 'pleasure'. There was a satanic, spiritual element too. A tug downwards which had nothing to do with any pleasure. More an attempt at recapture.

For our own prayer life

- To be converted, to be born again, is not to adopt a set of religious values or to decide to live by a Christian code, commendable though this might be. It is a direct meeting with God in His Spirit. It may be instantaneous or take time – but accept no imitations! God is really there and must be met.

- What draws someone to such an authentic meeting is not always what we might expect from our own experience, nor even what our (limited) Christian studies might seem to indicate. God's Spirit blows where He wills (John 3:8), most especially in answer to prayer. We just have to pray that 'by all means we can save some'.

- Passion is popular with God. Not extreme or unstable passion, but still passion. Passion is highly motivating. As with all biblical truths this applies to life as a whole. What we are passionate about gets done first! We should pray for a passionate heart for

God. Remarkably it seems that God even approves a passionate sinner more than a lukewarm Christian as the strong words in Revelation 3:15 indicate.

> 'To the angel of the church in Laodicea write:
> These are the words of the Amen, the faithful and true witness, the ruler of God's creation. I know your deeds, that you are neither cold nor hot. I wish you were either one or the other! So, because you are lukewarm – neither hot nor cold – I am about to spit you out of my mouth. You say, "I am rich; I have acquired wealth and do not need a thing." But you do not realise that you are wretched, pitiful, poor, blind and naked.' (Revelation 3:14–17)

CHAPTER FOUR

Foreigner

30. Set in workroom. Let
boys' clothes are ready
the afternoon.

4.30 Walk with boys.

_____

10 a.m. Quiet hour.

12.15. Set in workroom a
workroom duties.

12.30. bath for children

4.30 Set in workroom a
workroom duties.

_____

...sday:—
10 Quiet hour.

12.30 Set in workroom.
duties.

G eorg was to learn soon enough that while God's power was certainly greater than the Kaiser's, He tended to work things out in a different way and that, when dealing with believers, a preferred method is through their weakness. In later life a popular Bible passage of Muller's was, 'My grace is sufficient for you, for my power is made perfect in weakness.' Muller's was a strong personality – he was a strong man. But he had to learn God's ways – and his own limits. In a sense his real theological (knowledge of God) training had just begun.

In August 1828 he became ill. It started with a simple cold but became worse. He was disinclined to study Hebrew, showing just how ill he was, and took himself on long bracing walks to try and shake it off. But it was no use. An American professor had become his companion so, seeking a change of air and scene, they travelled together to Leipzig to visit the theatre. There Georg drank some iced water as refreshment which caused him to keel over dramatically during the show. It was only a faint but they returned hastily to Halle where he was diagnosed with a ruptured blood vessel in his stomach.

A few weeks in the country and he had recovered sufficiently to consider going to Berlin as the professor's guest. Despite his illness, Georg needed to pursue his release from conscription and, knowing this, the professor, having grown close to Georg, felt he could help. In fact he had been brought to a crisis point having seen Georg apparently so close to death in the Leipzig theatre. The professor had once been an active Christian but his faith had grown cold. Now he felt he had received a warning from God – and his early convictions were restored. It seems Georg's weakness was already admitting some of the grace of God into both their lives.

Berlin in 1829, though not yet the capital of a nation, was still a mighty city. The striking Brandenburg Gate declared to the world that its star was on the ascendant. The composer Franz Schubert, who had studied in Vienna under the famous Salieri, had moved there permanently from Austria; the botanist Johann Link was turning the Berlin Botanical Garden into a faculty to overtake Kew; and a certain freelance maths teacher called Georg Ohm was making some remarkable discoveries about electricity.

It was an exciting and vibrant place to stay. But the companions

were only part-time tourists. They were there in Berlin because they believed they could make a direct approach to the Kaiser and obtain the hoped-for military exemption. They were wrong. Every official avenue was closed. Every unofficial contact proved fruitless. And worse, their constant applications only highlighted Georg's attempt at draft dodging. It soon came to the crunch. Georg was ordered before the recruiters immediately.

He prayed and went forward ... and failed the medical. The Commanding General of the Military Depot interviewed him and sent him off to another surgeon for a second opinion. He confirmed the result. His lingering illness prevented his enlistment. The General, a Christian and supporter of mission work, then took great pleasure, though losing a potential recruit, in giving Georg his discharge *for life* in person. He even mentioned scriptures which he felt Georg would find useful when talking to Jews!

Georg saw God's hand in all of it and commented later, 'The King of Kings intended I should go to England!' He also reflected that throughout his life his times of personal inadequacy and weakness were very often times of God's particular activity. As for fighting, Georg never had to serve his country in warfare, but fight he did, most bitterly, for the rest of his life – for the orphaned and the poor, the lost and degraded, those too young and too weak to fight for themselves. He also battled in prayer for the souls of many, in a war from which he would never be discharged.

So, in March 1829, after saying goodbye to his father, now in Heimersleben where he had retired, apparently more resigned to his son's missionary vision, Georg travelled to Rotterdam, and when the river ice had broken, took the ferry to England.

If Berlin had been impressive, London was overwhelming. Capital city of a mighty empire which increasingly spanned the globe, entirely supported by sea trade, London was a port capital, with its focus centred on the arterial Thames where hundreds of ships lay in Tower Pool and the reaches below ready for lading, day and night. Sail was the order of the day, though steam was on the horizon. Stevenson's famous 'Rocket' engine ran at Rainhill that year and the first of the famous rail termini of the city would begin construction only eight years later, as would steam-paddle tugs. The first gas street lighting had been lit in Pall Mall twenty-two

OPPOSITE:
THE REICHSTAG
(TOP) AND THE
BRANDENBURG
GATE (MIDDLE
AND BOTTOM)
IN BERLIN

years before and now many metropolitan streets were similarly outfitted with the lighting that was 'ten times brighter than any oil lamp'.

The streets to the waterfront thronged with a wide mix of nationalities. Later Muller would become wholly familiar with the ebb and flow of the tide, the press of shipping on a large river and the peculiar cosmopolitan style of a seaport, when he made his home in Bristol. But for now, to the country boy from Saxony it was almost incredible. Berlin had a population of 200,000. London was already over one million.

The Regency period had ended when the Prince Regent became King George IV in 1820. A spendthrift and a waster as a youth, he now suffered the consequences, being overweight and addicted to drink and laudanum. He had a year to live. His legacy would be an era – and the architect John Nash's London: Regent Street, Regent's Park, Park Crescent, Trafalgar Square, Marble Arch and even some of Buckingham Palace.

But, though King of England, it would be hard to find anyone more German than 'gentleman George' – except perhaps his father 'farmer George', who it was said preferred his sows to his subjects for much of his reign. George IV was also King of Hanover, one of the many tiny European kingdoms which would eventually coalesce into the German nation. He took that job seriously.

Consequently all things German could be found at the British Court and this filtered down to the rest of the country. To be German was to be warm, cheerful, jolly and friendly, if rather eccentric; though to be Prussian was slightly different. Prussians were viewed then as many would view Germans now: precise and conscientious, if somewhat over regimented. But few in England could tell the difference and still less cared. Germans were welcome. Hence all Muller's co-students at the mission school were German (he complained about never being able to practise his English!) and he was able to travel around the country and be warmly received. His accent, far from putting people off, was attractive. In fact it sounded rather royal!

But it was a tense time in Britain. Not from war, as on the continent, but from riots. Still principally an agricultural nation, legal and technical changes on farms – mainly the introduction of 'enclosures' and the threshing machine – was causing major poverty in the labour force. The so-called 'Swing' riots erupted in 1830, smashing machines and intimidating farmers. Though harshly quelled these set the scene for an amendment of the Poor Law in 1834. This in turn established the workhouse, the grimmest structure on the later Victorian landscape, the existence of which was to haunt and spur Muller on all his life, as it did Charles Dickens and many other Victorian liberals.

The workhouse system was to be established as a last chance catch-all for destitute families, but inevitably hurt the most vulnerable – the children, often orphans, who could be expected to be put to work on the workhouse treadmill from the age of nine or ten. And to work all day. Factory or mine work was little better, young children commonly working in mills or underground an almost incredible one hundred hours a week. In contrast to the anti-slavery laws pushed through by the deeply Christian MP William Wilberforce in 1807 (slaves were fully emancipated in 1833) the equally committed Christian MP Lord Shaftesbury was unable to enact an end to this pitiless abuse of children until 1878.

At the missionary seminary Georg became George as he added an 'e' to adapt his Christian name to the culture (as had the king) though Muller stayed Muller not becoming Miller, the direct English equivalent. But he felt he was back at school. The regime was strict and the study, though interesting, unrelenting. He had spent all his life so far in study and really had had enough. But he pitched into it – and became ill again. He believed through too much study! As before, God seemed to be especially close as he became weaker. It was suggested he go to the West Country, to Devon, to try and recover and convalesce. It was the part of England destined to capture both his heart and life.

He actually thought he was dying and since he was quite happy 'to depart and be with Christ' he was not at all pleased to be told he was on the mend and should take a holiday! But he swallowed

> As before, God seemed to be especially close as he became weaker.

his disappointment and went down to Teignmouth, a hard three-day journey by stagecoach and horses from London. And there, no doubt, in the quiet seaside atmosphere of a village established on the coastal coal and clay trade he found a more gentle and familiar atmosphere than bustling, smoky, foggy London.

He could breath the clear Devon air and, as his health returned, enjoy cliff top walks amongst scenery the beauty of which he could scarcely have imagined even a couple of months before. And at last he could sleep. For he later noted how 'one sin in particular was brought to my mind' at this time – that being a failure to be thankful 'for uninterrupted refreshing sleep', which he had managed to enjoy during previous illnesses. But his last sickness had meant sleep 'for some nights had almost entirely fled from my eyes'. Muller was now sorry he had 'never heartily thanked God for it'.

And as he recovered he went to church. To chapel to be more exact. He had no connection with the Church of England and from his experience at the hands of the Lutherans he was happy to avoid any state religion, living in what he felt was true freedom in Christ. So he attended the opening of the Ebenezer Chapel, Teignmouth, effectively a 'free' church, and was greatly moved by the preaching. There he also formed a friendship with one who would become his right hand man in Bristol a few years later: a Scotsman by the name of Henry Craik. History and Muller really tell us very little about Henry Craik the man, but he and Muller quickly became fast friends – and that for almost forty years.

He, like Muller, was a young active believer with a calling – in his case to preach and minister in an independent church – which is exactly what he did alongside Muller in Bristol until his death in 1866. They were of the same age and the same heart. He was Jonathan to Muller's David, Dr Watson to his Sherlock Holmes, the writer Luke to the missionary Paul, Little John to his Robin Hood. A steady, loyal lieutenant who could be depended on to keep all the wheels turning, whilst the principal sparked about planning and persuading, capturing visions, hearts and bastions, and generally occupying the limelight. Muller's tribute to Craik was a 'beloved brother, friend and fellow labourer'. Without Craik, and in particular his support in effectively running the large Bethesda

HENRY CRAIK:
PHOTO FROM 1865 (LEFT) AND
FROM CTA FILM (ABOVE)

and Gideon Chapels in Bristol while Muller was occupied with the modest task of praying in a million pounds for new orphanages, Muller would have struggled to keep the plot. And he knew this. He leant hard on Craik over the years, for advice, prayer and friendship. And Craik never let him down. As Muller commented, 'for such, their reward will be very great in heaven'.

In Teignmouth Muller recovered his strength. And he had done some thinking. He had begun to have reservations about working with the London Society for Promoting Christianity Amongst the Jews. He wanted to work among the Jews right enough, but actually among all people, not just Jews. He was also increasingly unhappy about being tied to any society or organisation which had prescribed rules for ministry. Or which decided where that ministry should be undertaken – as the London Society certainly would when he had completed his training. He wanted to be wholly open to what he felt was the direct leading of God's Spirit and to freely and naturally interpret Scripture. He had already heard from

Henry Craik about a West Country man, a dentist from Exeter, just a few miles up river, who had given up his well-paid profession in response to a 'direct call from God to go as a Missionary to Persia'. This had impressed him so much he had written to his friends in Europe about it. He wanted to be like that. Not tied into a system.

ANTHONY GROVES

He liked free thinking. Little did he know that it was not only the thinking of former dentist Anthony Groves (a founder of the Brethren movement) that would influence his life. But he didn't know then that Groves had a sister.

Anyway George was heartily tired of studying and wanted to get out and do something. All of which, when he felt better, led him to politely offer the London Society an ultimatum which could be briefly summed up as: 'Bend the rules or I leave.'

In a letter which is a model of courteous restraint the Society replied: 'While the missionary sub-committee cordially rejoice in any real progress in Knowledge and Grace which may have been made under the teaching of the Holy Spirit they nevertheless consider it inexpedient that any Society employ those who are unwilling to submit themselves to their guidance with respect to missionary operations.' In other words the rules would stay and George would have to go. There was a dry, if gentle, concluding paragraph about what might happen if 'on mature reflection' Mr Muller changed his attitude, but apart from that, options with the Society were now at zero.

There was no rancour. It was a parting of the ways only. But it left George very much alone in a far country. But that, really, was the way he liked it. Not forgetting the help of the Holy Spirit, of course. But then George Muller was hardly likely to do that.

George Muller's life of prayer

Muller began to sense God's guidance early on. Being guided to 'foreign' England seems very strange, but for George 'to hear was to obey'. He never tried to rationalise his way out of guidance, but sought strongly to confirm unexpected feelings of guidance (such as a call to England) with Scripture study, the counsel of wise believing friends and much time in personal prayer. 'God *can't* be asking this of me' was not in his vocabulary.

This 'sensing of God's will first' before asking for things, became a main plank of his life of prayer and his teaching about prayer. Prayer to Muller was really a matter of deepening his relationship with God and God's enjoyment of a deepening relationship with Muller (to put it reverently). In other words, Muller knew perfectly well that God was not short on information about his needs. God knew them before he even mentioned them. And this applied both when he was a new Christian and later as a mature orphanage director. 'It was as though God was looking through our store cupboards' was how he used to put it later when he prayed for food for the orphans ... and the cupboards were empty. Nevertheless Muller noted that he often had to ask God many times for things. He put this down to God's need to stretch his faith, and sometimes the complexity of the (invisible) spiritual battle.

He learned too to love his Bible. He learned Hebrew and valued this for exposition. Greek also. His interest in Hebrew first drew him to consider ministry to the Jews. Hence his trip to London to start work for the London Society for Promoting Christianity among the Jews (now Church Mission to Jews). He saw reading the Scriptures as 'feeding the inner man', best done before prayer in the morning like a kind of spiritual breakfast.

His early illnesses taught him 'all things work together for good ...' (Romans 8:28) as a prime lesson of Christian life. Being threatened with TB not only got him medically rejected from Prussian army call-up, but his convalescence took him to Devon and the West Country, the region in which he was destined to stay for his life's work.

For our own prayer life

- We must try to accept guidance – when clear about it – however unusual it might seem; though getting it 'clear' may involve much personal prayer, discussion with other concerned Christians and close Bible study. As C.S. Lewis wrote of his Christ symbol, the lion Aslan in his Narnia Chronicles: 'Aslan is not a tame lion.' God is not wild in the wrong sense, but He often lacks convention and certainly comfort in what He asks of His followers. Career, home, even family ties, may be stretched, changed and challenged in the adventure of truly following God's call. As Muller and many others have found.

- We should *expect* to be guided. We are not groping hopefully in the dark. God had an individual plan for G. Muller, no question, though one which was likely to be revealed to him one step at a time. We are the same. And whilst many things may have gone wrong in our lives (we may be on plan C or D by now and can only thank God for a long alphabet), it is still firmly in place and tailored for each of us. But this plan may not be the gentle fulfilling Christian home service we have in mind. There is a desperate spiritual battle raging over the souls of humankind and that means casualties and cost. We must pray not only for guidance, but support and spiritual protection. And courage.

- What George did with his life was secondary to how deep he got into a relationship with God. The one interacted with the other of course, but it was the relationship – including the stretching and testing of his faith – which really mattered. We must pray always that we never lose sight of this. And the twists and turns of life, our triumphs and disasters (those two 'imposters' as Rudyard Kipling so wisely had it) will fall into their correct perspective against the overwhelming light of knowing Christ.

CHAPTER FIVE

Preacher

30. Set in workroom - ta[?]
boys' clothes are ready
the afternoon.

4.30 Walk with boys.

10 a.m. Quiet hour.

10.15. Set in workroom a
workroom duties.

12.30. train for children['s]

4.30 Set in workroom a
workroom duties. S

10 Quiet hour.

10.30. Set in workroom.
duties.

George returned to London in much better health both spiritually and physically. In fact he commented that his spirit was so uplifted by both the preaching he had heard and the response to the preaching he had done in Devon (despite a rich German accent) that it was 'almost like another conversion'.

Though at this time he was still querying his relationship with the London Society, he pitched in right away to nearby Jewish communities in the city, giving out small Bible excerpts in Hebrew and holding a popular all-comers Bible reading class for about fifty Jewish children. He thoroughly enjoyed doing it, but it wasn't all plain sailing. He records coolly that for his trouble he 'had the honour of being reproached and ill-treated for the name of Jesus' but that 'the Lord gave me grace never to be kept from the work by any danger or the prospect of any suffering'. The back streets of London were not the pleasantest of places to work at the best of times, as Charles Dickens was soon to make clear to a wider audience, and it took some courage to represent Christ in them, to Jews or anyone else for that matter. George soon noted that, whatever the spiritual uplift, front-line Christian service was never likely to be easy or comfortable.

He also stirred up the student body at his London seminary, holding late-night prayer and praise meetings in his room. We don't know what his fellow students in adjacent rooms thought as prayers continued energetically into the small hours, which Muller says they often did, but he mentions that he was often so taken up with these times of closeness to God that he felt compelled to wake his colleagues again at 6am to join him. There is no record of their comments about this either, but they were doubtless moved to hear that God had restored George's health and especially his ability to enjoy refreshing sleep after his recent illness.

That said, Muller's continual, intimate and frankly adoring attention to God was something which marked out the man throughout his life. If there is any 'secret' to his staggering success as a preacher, Christian philanthropist and social reformer, it is essentially this – his frequent and earnest meetings with God. His relationship with his Saviour was altogether too wonderful to be neglected. Sleep came a very poor second.

But, more practically – where ought he to go for his 1829 Christmas term break? Again the West Country called. He took the Exeter stage out of London for New Year to stay with his summer friends. These included the family of Anthony Groves, who was by now having a rather warmer festive season as an independent missionary in Baghdad, living there 'by faith in God alone for daily provision' – the lifestyle that had so impressed George when he had first heard about it.

The Groves and their friends were a cheerful, sincere and devotedly godly, almost family, group who were already out to break the mould of state church worship, much as the Methodists had done a century before, setting up a new denomination without deliberate intention but finding this the inevitable consequence of their fresh convictions. They met in small groups, studied the Bible intently as their rule of life and held closely to their belief that the essence of Christian faith was not form but a personal, spiritual relationship with Christ. Very pietist, in fact. Wholly authentic to Muller's experience and just up his street. He heartily endorsed these 'simple' Christian attitudes. Without really realising it George had joined the nascent Brethren (later Plymouth Brethren) movement then just beginning to spread across England and Ireland.

Brethren they may have been but it was actually someone's sister, along no doubt with the gently amused nudging of the Holy Sprit, that would keep the elegant, dashing, even rather exotic young Prussian focused on the West Country, there to find a female heart especially pleased to entertain him.

A London friend had given George the card of a lady who organised monthly preaching visits to Exeter for itinerant preachers. She had arranged such visits for Anthony Groves before he had felt called to work in the Middle East. Now there was a gap on the booking sheet and George was asked to fill it whenever he was in the area. The lady also arranged that on these visits he should stay at the Groves' former family residence, Northernhay House, now an infant boarding school run on behalf of new owners by Anthony's sister Mary. Later, after he had moved to the West Country, these monthly engagements in Exeter became weekly. Each time, he stayed at Northernhay House and found an

OPPOSITE:
GEORGE WAS
A POPULAR
PREACHER
WITH ALL HIS
CONGREGATIONS
(CTA FILM)

increasingly warm welcome there from its mistress.

So, whilst we cannot impute to George any more than his stated motives for leaving London for good, as he shortly did, it would be fair to say there were suddenly attractions in the south west ever so slightly above and beyond the call of missionary duty.

Mary, some ten years older than George, was a devoted Christian fully sympathetic to her brother's efforts overseas, and very accomplished, not only in the accepted 'female' skills of the day – music, painting, needlework and running a household – but she was also well read in languages including French, Latin and Hebrew. In addition she was a part-time scientist in astronomy.

Unlike his previous liaisons George set to this time to pray about the new girl in his life. He was keenly aware of the magnitude of any decision he might make, or want her to make – and of his troubled past. And this time he was prepared to wait. A very practical and godly way of facing the situation. Naturally a man of passion and action, he was beginning to learn God had lots of time, even if it seemed to George that matters ought to move more quickly. George's practical training course in theology was getting into its stride.

Something else he wanted to sort out in a hurry was a base for his line of work. The Society's decision made, George was now freelance, but with a burden for souls. He was a missionary in a foreign land and wanted some action. In this case God's timing was lightning quick. Within a few days of heading west and preaching in various of his old haunts he was asked by a member of the new Ebenezer Chapel, Teignmouth, to take over as minister or 'overseer'. He replied that he felt called to an itinerant ministry. As with Kipling's cat, he felt he should find all places alike to him. On the other hand there was clearly work to do in the area, somewhere he acknowledged that generally received 'little spiritual light'. Then there was his increasingly helpful comrade, Henry Craik. The two young men agreed on so many things. They might well become supportive local brothers-in-arms. And there was, of course, Mary Groves.

To decide what to do he prayed and then tried out what might be called in conventional warfare 'firing for effect'. He started to preach at Ebenezer Chapel. Unlike the early summer when he had been ill and his preaching had, he thought, been pretty uninspired, he now noted a good few of the congregation reacting markedly to his words – some by objecting strongly, others by responding very favourably. This happened several days in a row. He concluded: 'I could not explain it any other way than this, that the Lord intended to work through my instrumentality at Teignmouth, and that therefore Satan, fearing this, sought to raise opposition.' In other words, if the enemy was getting worried then he was probably shooting at the right target. He took the post.

He settled in Teignmouth and began work as a minister. A few of the objecting congregation left, but the church began to grow. People were converted. George, the missionary to England and not just Jews, was at last in business. In the business, as he often put it, of the kingdom.

> George the missionary to England and not just Jews, was at last in business.

By August he had come to another decision. He wrote to Mary Groves in Exeter. Would she marry him? One suspects, and hopes, that the actual proposal was worded less severely than George outlined later, with true Victorian decorum, in his own records. Whatever, it was almost certainly received with much warmth and emotion at Northernhay. Comments written later by George and others rather imply that she was clearly 'a suitable match' and 'appropriate to the task' and chosen 'from a full conviction' – rather as though they were two horses to be harnessed together between the shafts of a carriage! Given the work they were about to do, there may have been something in that, but there was very real love and affection between them too.

A sense of George's real sensitivity at the time, so different from his previous style of pursuing the women he wanted, may be gauged from the fact that, though he now stayed in Exeter at least once a week, he wrote and posted his proposal to Mary. It gave her time to consider freely. He knew full well that confronting her in person to ask for a decision might cause her to choose inappropriately or in haste. He was serious, and they would be in this for the long haul, and likely a tough one at that. He knew she needed space and no pressure from him to think and pray things through. To find a sense in herself of what God might want for them both. There was a difficult history here, too. Some years before, Mary had been proposed to by a military officer. The man was apparently 'wild and dissipated' and Mary had refused him. Heartbroken, and possibly deeply in debt, he had committed suicide. Mary had taken all this heavily on her spirit and was naturally nervous of personal involvement, especially with someone who had once been a very similar man. Had he changed? Yes, but had he changed enough? Enough for her? He had four days to wait to find out.

MARY GROVES, MULLER'S FIRST WIFE

In Exeter four days later, no doubt with heart pounding all the way to the front door, he went straight over to Northernhay after preaching. He need not have worried. When he turned up nervously on the step she was delighted to see him and pleased to accept him. Right away they knelt together and said a prayer to commit their future to God. They were married on 7 October 1830 at a nearby church in Exeter, took a private communion in Northernhay House and the afternoon stage to Teignmouth.

Mary proved a mainstay of his life and ministry from then on, despite being brought to death's door three or four times by illness over the next forty years. The Plymouth Brethren had, and still have, a particular perspective on women taking part in ministry and, by extension, the ministry of their men. They essentially feel that women ought not to be placed in leadership positions when men are present to take this responsibility. Muller and his chapel contemporaries all held to this and the women fell in line with it. But it did not mean that the women were weak, despised or downtrodden. Mary Muller ended her days effectively managing four massive orphan houses up to a year before her death in 1870, just living to see the fifth and final Muller house opened. Efficient, organised and tireless, she was by then also an expert accountant and complemented her husband's work in every way. And, as he did with Henry Craik, he leant on her heavily. He frequently acknowledged this debt. 'Her value to me,' he said, 'is beyond description.' Later, in a rare public admission of affection, he said, 'I never saw my beloved wife at any time, when I met her unexpectedly in Bristol, or even in the Orphan Houses, without my heart being delighted to do so. And she was equally pleased to see me. We had twelve months' happiness in the year.'

Under what many would consider to be massive pressures and publicity (both welcome and unwelcome) they made a marriage which worked, and worked well. Muller maintained it was because they had chosen 'to live for Christ', that they read the Bible frequently together and always prayed together at some moment in the day – as well as always having a lot of work to do! The fact was they were both passionate about the kingdom of God and closely shared each other's vision of how to extend it.

And this started at the beginning, when they were first married. Among many doctrinal points that George found his new position in Teignmouth forced him to think through and clarify, one of the most significant was his, or since his marriage, *their* mode of living. At the time most of a minister's income in a free or independent church derived from so called 'pew rents'. Those who came to church and sat in the pews were expected to pay for the privilege. And the better the seat the more a person had to pay. On top of this, ministers were allowed to accept donations, preaching expenses if travelling away, and one-off, usually seasonal, gifts, if people chose to give them, though this kind of support was uneven to say the least.

But George began to feel strongly that 'the gospel was not to be charged for'. As a missionary, someone who reached out into the community, was it fair to ask those who might be searching for the truth, or starting to find it at chapel, to pay to do so? Hardly. And a reading of the apostle Paul's letters seemed to confirm this. But if there was no pew rent – who would provide for the pastor and his new wife?

GEORGE AND MARY MULLER
(CTA FILM)

Mary, brother of 'pray-for-provisions' Anthony Groves, already knew the answer. Jehovah Jireh! The Lord will provide! Before leaving for Baghdad her brother had written a powerful and popular pamphlet called 'Christian Devotedness', advocating a 'just pray – and God will provide' principle. George had lapped it up in London along with his Hebrew. Was God now asking them to try it? They thought He might be.

So pew rents were abolished in Ebenezer Chapel, Teignmouth, and daily prayer for provisions was urgently commenced. And results awaited. George and Mary had confidence and faith. Surely it would work? To give God a helping hand they left out in the church a prominent box labelled 'for the support of Mr & Mrs Muller' with an agreement that it would be opened once a week by a church elder for their benefit.

The Mullers also instituted a personal policy to ensure it was only God's helping hand they received and that they did not manipulate others, intentionally or otherwise. They agreed that under no circumstances would they mention any need or want to church members, nor to anyone else. They would run down to the last penny, even their last farthing (quarter of a penny), and say absolutely nothing, even if pressed to do so. But they would not go into debt. If they were forced to do that they would conclude they had got it all wrong and would need to go back to the drawing board; but they did not expect to have to. Jehovah Jireh; God alone knew their circumstances. He would prompt others to provide just the right amount at the right time, they believed. He was intimately concerned with them. The Bible stated every hair on their heads was numbered. They settled down, in faith, to watch God in action.

George Muller's life of prayer

Muller never appeared disappointed when guidance did not seem to work out the way he, or others, might have expected. He very soon left the London Society (many would say precipitately) having felt rather 'constrained by their system' but soon settled into the church pastorship in Teignmouth, seeing in this move some greater plan. It took considerable flexibility of spirit to feel this way. Again his relationship with God seems to have been so intimate that apparent chopping and changing did not matter. In fact he was to be in Teignmouth only a couple of years before feeling moved to go to Bristol. And again he was rock sure this was the right move (despite tears and entreaties from his adoring Teignmouth congregation).

Preaching from a fixed script he found hard, but taking a text and speaking 'simply and directly' from it he found he loved, and it was something to which people responded. He did have a good theological training and background from Halle, of course, but always gave the Holy Spirit full credit for directing him during this kind of preaching. He spent his life in a close study of the Scriptures too and drew out principles which he then applied directly in his own life and then to any church where he had opportunity to preach or had pastorship. His foreign accent was an attraction and not an impediment. He felt especially 'helped' when preaching in English early on, but soon mastered the language fully, though apparently never losing his accent. He noted an advantage he sometimes had when preaching in that people would come to listen to him as a foreigner. As Jesus said, a prophet is often more honoured away from his homeland!

He also became a champion of reading 'just the scriptures & nothing but' and later said he regretted the time he had 'wasted' studying commentaries and Christian biographies as a young Christian when he could have been studying just the Bible. This is interesting if only because his own writings on Christian themes, presumably for the edification of others, ran to many hundreds of thousands of words!

Muller's marriage and first forays into the world of 'prayer for provision' are an early extension of his great lifetime conviction that God loved and cared for him, and each individual, on a person by person basis. There was no one-size-fits-all in the kingdom of God. He was also beginning to learn the value of time. Of waiting for things, and of God's precise timing.

For our own prayer life

• Continue to prayerfully expect the unexpected at the hand of God, particularly in timing. We should pray to know God's timing above our own schedules and timelines. His timing is definitely not ours! Not only experientially, but biblically – as in Psalm 90:4. and 2 Peter 3:8. And it is God's timing which matters.

> For a thousand years in your sight
>> are like a day that has just gone by,
>> or like a watch in the night.
> (Psalm 90:4)

> But do not forget this one thing, dear friends: With the Lord a day is like a thousand years, and a thousand years are like a day. The Lord is not slow in keeping his promise, as some understand slowness. He is patient with you, not wanting anyone to perish, but everyone to come to repentance.
> (2 Peter 3:8–9)

• Pray 'to become equipped' so far as possible to serve the kingdom.

> 'All Scripture is God-breathed and is useful for teaching, rebuking, correcting and training in righteousness, so that the man of God may be thoroughly equipped for every good work'
> (2 Timothy 3:16–17).

- And seek to study the Bible methodically, perhaps even take a Bible college course, at home or full-time, as God directs. Many people have, to their long-lasting gratitude, and others' benefit. Muller always valued and used the advantages given him by his education, academic ability, nationality and pastoral status (rather as the apostle Paul did his Roman citizenship and Jewish heritage), though his faith was rooted in none of these.

CHAPTER SIX

Pastor

30. Sit in nursery - Let
boys' clothes are ready
the afternoon.
30 Walk with boys.

day:-
a.m. Quiet hour.
15. Sit in nursery and
nursery duties.

12.30. Bath for children
4.30 Sit in nursery.
nursery duties.

sday:-
10 Quiet hour.
12.30 Sit in nursery.
duties.

Many years later, drawing on notes taken from his diary, Muller recalls that at the end of 1830, 'the Lord did not try our faith at the commencement, but gave us, first, encouragement'. The commencement being of the experiment of prayer-for-provision, following Anthony Groves' lead – and statements in his 'Christian Devotedness' pamphlet. But it is tempting to feel that it was only a thoroughly established George Muller, writing later with five orphanages and two churches under his belt, who could say that. At the time things were very much touch and go. All was certainly not calm waters and smooth sailing.

On 18 November their funds were down to '8s'. (To give a modern sense to the sums involved a housemaid would earn about 8s a week or just over £20 a year, a working man perhaps £30, a shopkeeper £80–£100 and an army officer £300 a year.) Prayers redoubled in earnest. A little later that day they were visiting a church member in the nearby estuarial village of Bishopsteignton. She put the question directly: 'Do you want any money?' George diverted the question, pointing out to her that he and Mary had resolved never to tell anyone about their needs, except in prayer to God. She protested that she had been disturbed over recent weeks, indeed the very last night, over promptings she felt were from God to give them money. Bravely George continued to steer the conversation away from money. He had concluded that 'if this was from God then she could not but give' and whatever he said or did would not affect matters. He was right. At the end of the visit she offered them 'two guineas' (£2 2s).

Between Christmas and New Year funds ran down to bare shillings again and George got down to pray. A few hours later a man who had come from Axminster, forty miles away, to see Muller about whom he had heard bad reports and so was determined to meet, was so impressed with his genuine lifestyle he gave him a sovereign (a £1 gold coin).

But the pressure was on. In the second week in January 1831, after continued prayers had seemingly produced nothing, Muller candidly confesses to feeling 'tempted to distrust' God. 'I began to say to myself I had gone too far in living in this way.' It was a bad moment for him. He wrestled with this (he felt as with the devil) for over five minutes, before feeling confident again. In fact, he records, 'Satan was immediately confounded' for when he got back to his room minutes later an Exeter lady had left them £2 4s.

In all of this the gifting box in the church proved a mixed blessing. When matters grew tight the Mullers would wonder how much might have been put in it to help them out. But, they argued with themselves, they had agreed never to make their wants known, so they felt they could not ask for the box to be opened as this would 'hinder the testimony'. Added to this, the church treasurer frequently failed to open the box on the agreed weekly basis. Muller wondered if this was because the sums in it were so embarrassingly small. As it turned out it was effectively opened monthly. One particularly tense time came when funds were low but he knew the box had been opened already. The treasurer had not yet counted the contents and passed the money on. Still Muller would not mention any need but prayed that the treasurer would feel strongly he ought to drop by with the funds. Four days later he did, just as the last pence in the Muller household were exhausted! He brought round £1 8s 6d.

Muller's precision in such matters, even as far back as 1831, his records of the sums given to him for his family and the work he undertook, is wholly typical of the way he approached money. He

MULLER IN HIS STUDY
(CTA FILM)

was never dismissive of good accounting or good business practice. Over the years he went to endless lengths to record every single transaction, down to the last farthing, in his every dealing. Much of his many diaries, taken up with page after page and column after column of figures, often compiled by Mary as well as himself (when later orphanage funds are involved) showed, in Muller's words, 'God's abundant faithfulness'.

He had learned well at the feet of his father how good accounts should be kept and, given the weight he intended should be placed on his testimony to the blessing of God, how good accounts should be presented to critical analysis. For, from this time onwards, he was to be under a spotlight of distrust. Time and time again, he had to be prepared to show his precise and detailed book-keeping to others to prove he was not involved in some swindle or scam, that funds were not being manipulated or blackmailed out of people, spirited in from abroad out of some mysterious German inheritance, or siphoned from the collection plate of his increasingly full churches. He had, he knew, from the first weeks of this Christian experiment, taken on the devil at a battlefront where the fighting was likely to be of the hottest. The love and lure of money, as the apostle Paul wrote to Timothy, was a 'root of all evil' and so any apparently unusual dealings with it, such as 'praying for it' would draw Muller into the firing line from many quarters. He had to be absolutely, rigorously, transparent.

But, even in a fallen world, sub-let as it were to the master accuser, Muller held Christ, *his* Master, to have triumphed at the cross and thus be conqueror in all things. Money, lightly held and readily given, not loved and lusted after, could be a tool for good. And, with God's help – and daily double-entry book-keeping – he was setting out to prove it.

So in the winter and spring of 1831 George learned the style cycle that was to become his way of life for the future. Funds would run low, prayers would become urgent, and then at the last minute money would be given to keep things going. Nothing was regular, nothing was even. Sometimes a gift was larger and would last several weeks, sometimes it was a few pence for only a matter of days, or even hours. In June he recorded: 'We have been praying repeatedly for money ... funds are now down to 3s ... and this morning we have 9d left ... only a little butter for ourselves and visitors, but we have said nothing.' A tense (for Muller) morning meeting with church members passed, then, without warning, the treasurer opened the support box. He gave Muller the money right away, counting it out on the spot (£1 8s 10½d), saying he and his wife had been unable to sleep the night before due to worry about the Mullers' situation! Muller concludes the story by saying that the most striking point to him was that he had been praying specifically for the box to be opened. He had, of course, not hinted at their depleted circumstances.

> Funds would run low, prayers would become urgent, and then at the last minute money would be given to keep things going.

Among free churches and the growing Brethren movement a tradition had developed that when a man was preaching away from his home church he would be given expenses for his trip which was usually a little above the genuine travel costs, in gentle thanks for the service provided. Muller, again feeling the gospel should never be charged for, refused these. But he would often find, en route back to Teignmouth, that coins had been slipped into his pocket, or into Mary's bag if she had come with him. Such persistent contributors he concluded, after some prayer and discussion, were entitled to give such gifts as they wished, and so the money should be kept, as ever thanking God.

A more complex matter was whether to keep shop accounts with grocer, butchers, bakers, etc. This was the local trading norm and such an account would be run up daily or weekly and be settled each month. It was standard shopkeeper's practice. But the Mullers decided not to go along with this, as they felt that daily was the bread they should ask for and expect to receive and daily they should pay for it. They did not dismiss the practice of accounts entirely out of hand (though strongly recommended others to question it) but felt that they, in their special circumstances, might lay themselves open to spending more than they ought if credit was available. 'Paying with ready money' became their policy and Muller often cited Romans 13 verse 8 (leave no debt outstanding ...) in support of this.

In fact he tells one story about receiving daily bread quite literally: Sunday 27 November 1831. Funds were again low – down in fact to 2½d. Muller had prayed a number of times about this as their cash had steadily reduced. After dinner he said again the Lord's Prayer with special emphasis on the 'daily bread' section – meaning that they actually needed bread for that very evening, though he knew that even if money somehow appeared all the shops would be closed on a Sunday. As he was praying there was a knock at the door and a woman came in, one of the poorer members of the congregation, who proceeded to offer them some of her own dinner plus 5s given her by another local woman, also poorly off. She also brought a large loaf! 'Thus,' says Muller triumphantly, 'the Lord not only literally gave us bread, but also money!'

Taking stock on the morning of 31 December 1831 he noted that they only had 10s in hand but by the end of the day that too had been spent and given away. Thus, he noted, 'not a single farthing remained.' But his annual accounts recorded that they had received, without a word to anyone, £131 18s 8d, plus about £20 in goods and services throughout that year. Of course quite a lot of that they had given away, but he still noted that the regular annual salary from pew rents which he and his wife had abandoned was considerably less than this. 'I have,' he concludes, 'not served a hard Master.'

Within days they were back on their knees as they had no rent money for the second week in January! And, as ever, it was given to them at the eleventh hour – quite literally – at 11 pm the night before it was due. God, he found, would provide, but always at the expenditure of prayer, and the exercise of faith. And to His own timetable.

Very soon over two years had passed in Teignmouth, the second much like the first, though severe stomach illness and bleeding again shadowed the early part of it. But, unlike the last time, when he felt he would have been content to die, he now felt he still had work to do in this world before moving on to the next and so hung on in faith for healing (and for a rather desperate day of preaching while the bleeding was at its height). And healing came. He had also begun by now to pray for healing in others, though he always counselled the advice of a good doctor too where illness was involved. God, he believed, worked in many ways for the good of humankind. But he acknowledged, too, that healing seemed apparently to come to many that he had prayed for, though this was not a ministry to which he felt specifically called. And he developed a sense, he called it a 'gift of faith', for those he felt he should pray for to be healed, and to persist in doing so, whilst others he felt he could only legitimately 'commend to God in his mercy'. This was clearly again a very personal matter dependent on his intimate relationship with God; in fact when it came to his dying son, as yet to be born, it could hardly get much more personal. But throughout his life he maintained he could sense God's will, after prayer, often much prayer – and waiting – and was then led to act and live accordingly. It was his rule of life.

In Teignmouth other matters were firming up in his thinking, as well as in his spirit. He became convinced of the importance of baptism as an adult, as a sign and confirmation of a Christian's conversion, and that this should be a matter of complete submerging in water. Accordingly, he and Henry Craik went forward for this. He had already brought in weekly celebrations of the Lord's Supper, Holy Communion with bread and wine, at Ebenezer Chapel, including in these times opportunities for any man in the congregation to contribute to the meeting with a prayer, Bible reading or comment. He felt this an important biblical principle indicating that every believer was effectively a priest, entitled to a personal, redeeming, link with God. Muller himself saw his role in the chapel as one of leadership simply as a pastor or co-ordinator.

To Muller perhaps the most motivating and energising of all his fresh understandings was his new perception of the 'last days' or 'end times'. His reading of Revelation and other Bible books had led him to the conclusion that the second coming of Christ could happen at any time with little warning and also that this might happen sooner rather than later. This thinking made him increasingly ashamed of his former wish for death when last ill, as there now seemed to him so much more to be done before Christ returned. He had to get on with it. Though discussion about interpreting the end times was something of a hot potato in Muller's day (and more recently too), it is typical of him that he found it spurred him into Christian activity and not, as the apostle Paul had warned a young Timothy to avoid, into 'controversies' and 'meaningless talk'.

In April 1832 Henry Craik had returned from a month's preaching in and around the large port city of Bristol, still in the south west of England but 100 miles to the north of Teignmouth on the west rather than the south coast. He had had a successful preaching tour there among the businesslike and cosmopolitan residents. It held, as he wrote to George, 'fields ripe for the harvest'. George, already beginning to feel that his time in Teignmouth was drawing to a close, thought he might perhaps be being called to be one of the reapers. In fact Henry, having gone back once more to the city, soon wrote to invite him to do just that – to move north and take on a church together with Henry. He prayed over this into the summer, making a preaching tour of Bristol himself to help him decide. By May he had. He and Mary would go. Gideon Chapel in Bristol had decided to accept Henry and him as joint ministers, at no salary and for no fixed term, abolishing the pew rents as they had asked (which had also been the agreed deal at Teignmouth, and at nearby Shaldon village where Henry had been working). Another chapel, called Bethesda, was also debating whether to ask them to help out in similar vein, if the present church members could find another year's rent for the building. They did this a month after the Mullers moved.

So, at the end of May, amid much crying and lamenting, he and Mary visited all fifty or so members of Ebenezer Chapel (there had been under twenty in 1830) at their homes in Teignmouth to say a personal goodbye, and to explain why they felt God's call to move on.

Then on the evening of 23 May they set out for Bristol. The city from which Muller was destined to put his personal faith on the map – the map of the world.

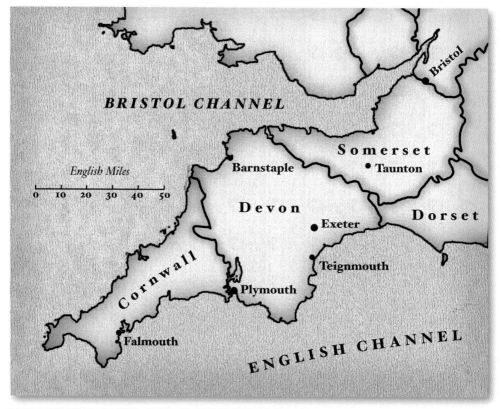

SOUTHWEST ENGLAND, INCLUDING THE LOCATION OF TEIGNMOUTH AND BRISTOL

George Muller's life of prayer

Despite an inevitable increase of focus on it at this stage in the story, Muller's prayer life was *not* just asking for things or (later) orphans' supplies in order to be comfortable or 'keep going'. Prayer was an integrated part of *all* of his life. Of course he needed to support himself in Teignmouth in order to continue his ministry. But it was the latter that was really important to him, not the support as such. The same applied to Bethesda Chapel in Bristol later and funds for overseas missions, The Scriptural Knowledge Institution etc.

He always coupled prayer with active faith. 'Believing faith' was his expression. This is easy to say but more difficult to explain. How much faith is needed? To a certain extent this kind of experience builds on experience. The more you find your prayers are answered the more you are likely to exercise 'believing faith' as you offer them up. Clearly, believing faith depends on a sense of understanding of what God has in mind anyway. Muller believed in taking time in prayer to sense what he felt to be the will of God *first*. He didn't start by asking. He tried to sense what it would be right to do, what should be done, what to ask for. Then he prayed for these resources. He prayed for what he felt God *already wanted* to provide for a work.

This 'sensing God's will' was in many ways a wholly individual experience and often operated over some considerable time. Answers and guidance were judged against his reading of the Bible (which was subject to his own interpretation, as he often made clear, though it was straightforward enough) and talked over with his trusted Christian friends, most notably his wife and Henry Craik. Overall though it was a sense of 'peace in his spirit' which he finally looked for before deciding on actions and thus what he should pray for.

This had two clear effects.

A. He would persevere in prayer. Once committed it was, to him, just a matter of keeping going until the floodgates opened.

B. He would hold on for a long time. Longer, in faithful hope, than many would. In fact for as long as it took. This was based on his early Teignmouth experiences of God favouring answers at the last minute. He said he could keep calm in these circumstances because he had the 'mind of God' clear at the time. To him, his petitioning prayer was just the last stone slab on a pathway of Christian living. The main end of it being not only the provision of whatever he was asking for but a deepened relationship of faith. And – which was also vital – a remarkable witness.

For our own prayer life

• We need to pray to learn to persevere, and not only in prayer. To keep on keeping on, to try, try, try again. It is a familiar lesson, but to set our hand to the plough and not look back is hard and demands great determination and self control.

• We must pray to learn to persevere without apparent support or encouragement. It is not hard to climb even a tough hill with others leading or with supporters cheering and approving. But to go alone, against worldly advice, or even well-meaning, but perhaps short-sighted, Christian advice is much harder. Especially when night falls. But it is a part of discipleship and of the faith-testing process. The pilgrim's personal journey. The bottom line being, 'I am with you always, even to the very end of the age' – the last words of Matthew's Gospel (Matthew 28:20).

• We should try in prayer not just to list our needs but to discover what it is that God has in mind for us to pray for and to do. To consciously ask Him what He has in mind for us to do and to ask. And to try and develop an attitude of mind that says, not as on the T shirt, WWJD (What Would Jesus Do?) but WWJHMD (What Would Jesus Have *ME* Do?). As ever, it is down to the faithful relationship.

CHAPTER SEVEN

30. Sit in workroom – Let
boys' clothes are ready
the afternoon.
p.30. Walk with boys.

_____

sday:–
6 a.m. Quiet hour.
12.15. Sit in workroom &
workroom duties.
19.30. bath for children
6.30 Sit in workroom &
workroom duties.

_____

sday:–
11 Quiet hour.
19.30 Sit in workroom.
duties.

The year 1832 was perhaps not the best time for anyone to be moving to Bristol. For a start there was the rioting. October 1831 kicked off a year of riots in several of England's major cities. The atmosphere was highly charged and many feared there was about to be a French revolution-type bloodbath. In some cities they weren't far wrong.

At the centre of this was the Reform Act, a change in the Parliamentary system which would take the vote away from the aristocracy and give it, or at least share it, with more of the people, effectively the new industrial middle class. It was urgently needed, and those politicians who could sense unrest brewing remembered France's terrible social experiment and were desperate to adjust the representative balance before heads began to roll.

But it was stalled in Parliament. A new prime minister, Earl Grey, had at last ousted the Duke of Wellington, a good soldier but die-hard aristocrat, and got the bill through the Commons only to have it voted out in the House of Lords by Wellington and his cronies (including a sizable number of bishops). This most incensed people in the fast-growing cities, who therefore remained massively unrepresented. National riots followed. In Bristol mobs burned the Mansion House, Bishop's Palace and Custom House. The twelfth-century cathedral barely escaped the same fate. Following a reading of the Riot Act by the mayor (who then gave the mob the slip disguised as a washer woman) dragoons had to sabre their way across the city to restore order. They killed over 500. For days blazing buildings lit up the countryside for miles around.

The political fallout from this and the other city riots pushed the Reform Act through in June 1832. This would matter very much to Muller for, even if he avoided the riots, these reforms paved the way for the 1834 Poor Law Amendment – and the institution across the country of the hated workhouse.

Port cities in 1832 were also pretty unsafe on health grounds. Hard on the heels of the riots came an epidemic of cholera. Originating in the Far East it rapidly moved across Europe and, hosted by sewage-tainted drinking water, standard in most cities of the day, the disease hit the United Kingdom hard in June spreading westwards from the port of Sunderland. Over 20,000

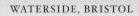
WATERSIDE, BRISTOL

were to die.

Muller, who throughout his life deliberately and probably wisely, avoided commenting on politics, says nothing about the rioting, but much about the cholera. It was his, and Henry's, first pastoral challenge.

In August he wrote '... great numbers die daily in the city. Who may be next God alone knows. Just now at ten in the evening the funeral bell is ringing. It rings almost all the day.' Despite their personal fears Muller and Craik bravely chose to visit the members of their new congregations of Bethesda and Gideon Chapels to pray with the frightened folk and offer what comfort they could – all the while wondering, with every contact, if the disease was going to fasten on one or either of them. 'Except the Lord keep us this night, we shall no more be in the land of the living tomorrow!' Muller exclaims.

Cholera was a deadly mystery, a dark angel. With death all around, they could only pray. Henry Craik recorded that a neighbouring couple (the Mullers and Craik were now living in the same house) had each contracted the disease and died within twenty-four hours of each other. The two young pastors called a special prayer meeting and continued it every morning from 6am to 8am at Gideon Chapel. Two or three hundred people, many not church members, attended.

It was a harsh and challenging welcome to their new home. But the epidemic finally passed and in October the duo called for a service of thanksgiving that the city had been spared a worse fate and that a good number had been brought to face their own mortality by the sweeping death – and come into faith as a consequence. 'How merciful in its results has this heavy judgement been to many!' Muller concludes, while lamenting that a good many who had come to the church meetings had lapsed back into their old ways once the danger had passed. As ever, no matter what the circumstance, Muller never blamed God. Even for cholera. Hard to understand perhaps. But he always accepted that his loving Father did only what was best. God was only the 'author of great mercies'. It might not look like it, but that was the way it was. And he was shortly going to have to face, in his own life, a very fierce assault on that belief.

At the thanksgiving meeting George was personally full of gratitude for, right in the midst of the chaos, Mary had borne him a daughter. She herself had become ill, though not with cholera, and at one point had seemed so close to death that Muller had felt called to stay up a whole night to pray for her. She recovered and a month later Lydia was born. Both mother and daughter were doing well.

Almost two years passed and the congregations in both Gideon and Bethesda Chapels had risen remarkably – by over 150, with still more having come to faith under their combined ministries (Muller and Craik would preach week and week about) who had then joined other churches. Mary had given George another child, a son, Elijah, and the team had set up a new mission support enterprise.

The Scriptural Knowledge Institution for Home and Abroad was effectively a fund-focusing system. It meant that money could be directly put into providing Bibles and portions of Bibles for local day schools and adult schools (not necessarily Christian ones, but where Christian teachers were identified and were teaching from a godly viewpoint) and Sunday schools and other mission enterprises not directly connected with the two chapels. Craik and Muller understood the central position education had in drawing young people to consider personal faith and wished to provide the means locally and nationally – and, eventually, internationally, for SKI also became the means of supporting many overseas missionaries. Even in the first year £57 was sent overseas to support missionaries.

The now standard Muller and Craik 'pray and pay' approach was locked into the establishing statement of SKI, including never appealing for funds, never running up any debts and receiving no patronage from non-believing institutions or individuals. In this missionary work 'God alone shall be our Patron,' wrote Muller in his diary in February 1834.

After a break the next line reads: 'Today we have only one shilling left.' Not much had changed since Teignmouth. Nor would it ever. Daily prayer and daily provision, no matter how grand the plan or mission, how large various church congregations grew or, in due course, how many orphanages were built and paid for, the

BETHESDA CHAPEL,
ST GEORGE STREET, BRISTOL
(DESTROYED 1942)

lifestyle of this type of provision seemed to remain the same.

The week before his death in early March 1898, aged 93, faced with massive outgoings on churches, five new orphanages (2,000 children and 600 staff) plus thousands of pounds committed to SKI Bible products and missionaries home and abroad, Muller wrote: 'The income today, by the first two deliveries was £7 15s 11d. Day by day our great trial of faith and patience continues, and thus it has been more or less now, for twenty-one months, yet, by Thy grace, we are sustained.'

That after receipts over sixty-eight years running close to £1.3 million – at nineteenth-century prices! His precise notebooks, kept in neat ledger entry style, record every penny, every farthing of income, right to the end. The extreme tension and the entire confidence of his faith lasting to his final breath. A trust absolute in a God whom he took to be never less than wonderful in every way. Under this is his final note two days later: 'The Lord has refreshed our hearts! This afternoon came in for the Lord's work, £1,427 1s 7d, as part of a legacy from Mrs ECS.'

At last, as George ever expected, after a test of faith God had provided for their needs. He had again proved faithful. And, in a sense, so had George. For after his death it was found that this legacy money, along with many other similar gifts large and small down the years, had been given to Muller solely for his own personal use. And, as he so often did, he had passed it on directly to the work.

Perhaps back in 1834, in the early days, he imagined this might one day change. That, after everything was set up along the lines God no doubt had in mind, when enough people had been converted and were attending the churches and supporting the work, then matters might ease, or at least regularise. There would grow up a natural inertia for the giving. The various Christian works would be established and well publicised (though there would never be any direct appeal) and donations would become regular and routine. Extra sums for expansion and outreach would flow in naturally and all could be anticipated and orderly. But for George this never happened (though he encouraged regular giving and preached the value of it). Partly, no doubt, because he felt he should keep on pushing the envelope of his and Craik's ministry, and so needed greater and greater sums of money for the operation, but mainly, he believed 'because God wanted always to try our faith'.

That he found this a great burden at times is unquestionable. He confesses in his diary: 'For several weeks I have had very little communion with the Lord. I long for it. I am cold. I have little love for the Lord.' He then breaks out in an almost desperate prayer to become more loving and fervent in spirit towards God. The next day he records: 'By the mercy of God I was today melted into tears on account of my state of heart!'

And with that his prayers seem to have been answered so profoundly he sat down the next day to write out the first draft of a paper setting up the Scriptural Knowledge Institution! His honesty and passion were always compelling. And God seemed to respond to it. By the end of that year he and Mary had received, in faithful fits and starts, £230 in cash and an estimated £60 in kind, including gifts of hats, coats, tailor's services for new suits, vegetables and bread left on the doorstep, and so on. In all a good cut above a normal young minister's income though a lot was given away. The Mullers had moved on by then as Henry Craik had recently married. Their new home was at 21 Paul Street, High Kingsdown in Bristol. Their carpeting and furnishings were all provided, unasked, by the church.

21 PAUL STREET, HIGH KINGSDOWN

But a trial of faith of a different sort was coming upon George. He had returned to Germany briefly to assist Anthony Groves, now back from Baghdad, in recruiting German Christians for further missionary work there among the German community and also to see his own father. Johann was delighted to see him in Heimersleben, parting from him afterwards with 'many tears'. Also delighted to see him was his old mentor Dr Friedrich Tholuck when he visited Halle. And of course the Doctor at the university was a natural contact to sound out potential missionaries. On travelling back he notes how moved he was, particularly as he passed Wolfenbuttle and Brunswick, to see how far God had brought him since travelling that road before.

Within a few days of landing back in Bristol, Anthony and Mary's father had become ill. Over the next six weeks his health gradually declined. By June Muller notes he considered his father-in-law's end was near. Mary was distraught. Then, as if not burdened enough by the approaching death of her father, she learned that her only son, their beloved little Elijah, now just two, had been diagnosed as dangerously ill with 'inflammation of the chest'. Daughter Lydia too was unwell. It was a time for George to make extraordinary exertions in prayer.

> It was time for George to make extraordinary exertions in prayer.

Mr Groves senior died on 22 June 1835, to be remembered not only as the father of the first Brethren missionary but also the father of one who was jointly to set up and run, in extraordinary circumstances, homes which would save the lives of many thousands from the horrors of the Victorian streets, and inspire a generation of others to do likewise. Mary grieved, and continued to tend her sick children. George continued to preach. And to pray. But, four days later, on 26 June, in the small hours, with his father and mother by his tiny cot side, little Elijah succumbed to pneumonia. Where was the successful prayer warrior now? What had become of his passionate entreaties? Had God not heard this time or, more cruelly, had He heard but not chosen to answer? Or, more cruelly still, had the all-powerful One chosen to answer by deliberately dashing all their hopes? In the circumstances these might seem legitimate questions.

But Muller didn't see it like that. He records the moment with great gravity and simplicity, echoing almost exactly the tone of Job in the Old Testament: 'The Lord gives and the Lord takes away, blessed be the name of the Lord.'

Muller said all he felt he could do was pray that night that 'The Lord's holy will be done concerning the dear little one.' He recorded that much of this time he spent praying for his wife – that she should be supported in her trials, and that if their son was to be taken from them then it should happen quickly to spare him suffering. 'It was but two hours after that,' he records, 'the dear little one went home.'

He then just prayed, 'May the Lord grant that these afflictions be not lost upon us.' Three days later there was a joint funeral and little Elijah's body was interred with that of his grandfather. Muller preached, he said, 'comfortably'. He was not being hard-hearted in all this. He was perhaps more able to accept God's will as he saw it because he felt he had good cause to do so. God loved him and had redeemed him. This present life was not the end and was never going to be a matter of striving for longevity, security and comfort. It was just a preparation for the life to come. His son had simply gone on ahead. He would see him again, in due time. It must also be said that infant mortality in those days was very, very common, with upwards of a third of children born dying as babies or toddlers. In some ways it was to be expected. But the Mullers still felt the loss deeply. They just did not blame God for it.

It is worth noting that in an era when the average family, even the most wealthy, numbered around eight children (Queen Victoria, yet to be queen, bore seven) the Mullers had no more children of their own after Elijah's death. Perhaps Mary simply could not, which would have made her personal loss that much harsher. Or perhaps it was a function of the fact that, shortly after this tragedy, the Mullers' familial love would be directed wholly towards a great many children, not of their own bloodline it is true, but who would still need, urgently, the protective care of a mother and father.

George Muller's life of prayer

The loss of his son was obviously a very great personal blow, but Muller said about it two things we might not expect. The first was that he had not felt 'called to pray' for his son's recovery, and the second that his tears at his son's death were as much of joy as of grief.

Perhaps the second is more easily understood, as tears reflect all types of great emotion and in Muller this was allied to his strong conviction that his little child was now 'safe with Jesus', the Saviour whom Muller himself often stated he loved more than life itself. Jesus' statement regarding children, 'of such is the kingdom of heaven' (Matthew 19:14) was a great comfort to him at the time. He accepted, apparently wholly, the need for God to take some children 'home to himself' and was content that He did so even though he loved little Elijah. He believed fully the Pauline tenet 'to live is Christ, to die is gain' and so actively and honestly looked forward to death (if his Lord did not return before for His second coming as outlined in Revelation, something he always felt very possible).

Without seeming harsh, it should also be remembered that the child mortality rate in Europe was generally much higher than we are now used to and that international pandemics such as cholera were more common (hence the large number of orphans in Bristol after the 1832 outbreak). To lose up to a third of a family's children before the age of twelve was not abnormal. The author Charles Dickens, a contemporary, was one of eight children, two of whom died in their first year.

Muller's first comment helps us a little to understand some of his attitude towards petition in prayer. In *A Narrative of Some of the Lord's Dealings with George Muller Vol 1* he outlines an understanding of what he calls two areas of faith – and their effect on his ability to pray, faith and prayer being almost two sides of the same coin to Muller.

He says that for him there was a Gift of Faith and a Grace of Faith.

'The Gift of Faith' he defines as a gift (to him) of understanding that God would do something, or enable him to believe something would be done in answer to his prayers. This Gift of Faith as he called it was for special circumstances – such as a sense that God wanted someone healed, or spoken to or met. This Muller felt was always something that, though important, would not be a sin if he did not do it. Quite why he put it like this we do not know, except to contrast it with what he called the Grace of Faith which would be something like believing God would provide all his needs, provided he seek first God's kingdom, etc. Doubting this Muller would call sin as he asserts this is a scriptural promise (Matthew 6:33).

These may seem over-complicated or even rather like hair-splitting to us, but Muller felt the difference was highly significant. Daily he would happily ask for provisions as we have seen. To him they were the subject of a biblical general promise. God, as it were, had already authorised prayer for this so it was just a matter of getting on with it. But the praying for a healing, or funds for a second orphanage, or to meet the right church worker just in time to learn important church business was different. It demanded, in Muller, a sense in his heart that it ought to be prayed for, that God wanted it prayed for. That the burden to pray had been specially given. A Gift of Faith. Evidently, as we have already seen, this is very subjective, though Muller found it real, as his relationship with God was real. He had felt called to stay up all night and pray for his wife in 1832, who had then been healed, but not called to do the same for his son three years later. All he felt he should do then was pray that God's will would be done, quickly.

He comments too that he had prayed unconditionally for a number of people to be healed over the years. And they had. But he and his closest allies, eg Craik, his wife Mary and daughter Lydia, continued to suffer serious illnesses on and off throughout their lives. He lost two wives, and his daughter when in her fifties. Paul, too, had his unhealed thorn in the flesh.

For our own prayer life

- The often-quoted prayer: 'God grant that in life I may have the courage to change the things I can, the grace to accept the things I cannot and the wisdom to know the difference' contains a sense of Muller's meaning. We need to learn to pray not for what we want (however desperately and however much we feel justly entitled to it) but for what God has in mind. The wisdom to know ... To ask first for God's opinion rather than just His action.

- Pain and suffering are a routine part of life, even in (some would say especially in) the life of faith. The apostle Paul had a 'thorn in the flesh' which he prayed about but it was not removed, though he had healed many others. We do not know why. The devil has a harsh grip on this fallen world. It is as important to pray for patience, for endurance and for cheerfulness under painful circumstances, as it is for healing. Such qualities, says the apostle, are crucial. See Romans 5.

   > Therefore, since we have been justified through faith, we have peace with God through our Lord Jesus Christ, through whom we have gained access by faith into this grace in which we now stand. And we rejoice in the hope of the glory of God. *Not only so, but we also rejoice in our sufferings*, because we know that suffering produces perseverance; perseverance, character; and character, hope. (Romans 5:1–4, my italics)

- We must be prayerfully ready 'to walk with death' at any time, even in our safe and protected society. Tragic illness and accident can strike at any time, among friends, family or work colleagues. As Christians, whoever we are, we have significant responsibility in these situations to reach out with care and comfort, to advise and to pray for those facing death, or for someone dealing with the death of a loved one. We must pray for sensitivity, for love and patience and an extra ability to serve someone facing this extremity.

CHAPTER EIGHT

Philanthropist

30. Set in workroom. See!
boys' clothes are ready.
The afternoon.

4.30 Walk with boys.

...sday:—
11 a.m. Quiet hour.
19.15. Set in workroom a...
workroom duties.
12.30. ...for children
4.30 Set in workroom a...
workroom duties. ...

...sday:—
11 Quiet hour.
12.30. Set in workroom.
...duties.

George had been thinking about Dr Francke. His recent visit to Halle had once again taken him past the mighty buildings of the Franckesche Stiftungen (the Francke Foundation), the eighteenth-century orphanage, school and workshop complex apparently 'prayed into being' by the pietist professor. He had also run across a biography of the man back in Bristol which he had re-read and been much impressed by. Was God turning his mind in this direction for a reason? He set himself to prayer.

He had felt for the abandoned children of the city streets ever since coming to Bristol. His diary is full of comments about the poverty of so many he met (to whom he usually tried to give something) and in particular the orphaned children, many made so by the recent cholera epidemic. Now, after the Poor Law had been amended in 1834, their only recourse was the parish workhouse – a 'benefit' scheme specifically designed to deter people. Its dour reputation was supposed to repel. A growing middle-class society desperate for cheap labour in its factories had decided that any kind of worker was preferable to someone 'living off the parish', and so branded anyone who did not work as idle. And as most children were expected to work by the age of eight or nine they were included.

For those whose circumstances were so bad they were forced into the workhouse, all they did was work – usually on a treadmill, or hand crushing bones (for fertiliser) or stones (for masonry), earning a pint of gruel and a few ounces of bread and water daily and a bed for the night. The clothing provided was striped like a prison uniform. For children there was no education system, no chance or hope of betterment, no health care and, above all, no love. The system provided a bare minimum to those viewed as lazy scroungers. Individual difficulties, disablement and other problems were never considered. The older system, geared to agricultural communities, had worked as a poverty 'top-up' to those well known locally to be in need. But in a city-based industrial society that was outdated – and now outlawed.

So, many preferred the streets. At least there you could steal, cut and run. There was freedom of a sort – and comradeship, and if disease and death struck, well, it was a short life for most anyway.

'I longed to set something before the children of God whereby they might see that he does not forsake, even in our day, those who rely upon him,' wrote Muller in November 1835.

So George wanted to help. But, as he had written, he wanted to do something else. He wanted to show that God could provide. That He was there, that He still cared. Plus, mindful of Francke, he wanted to see if an orphanage could be run along the lines he had set out – very similar to those established for his and Henry's ministry: the 'pray and pay' system. No appeals, no statement of needs, no debts, but many prayers and a full, transparent account rendered annually. He wrote:

> The first and primary object of the work will be that God might be magnified by the fact that the orphans under care will be provided with all they need only by prayer and faith without anyone being asked by me or my fellow labourers whereby it may be seen that God is faithful still and hears prayer still.

It was a courageous hope. Making a living as a popular preacher was one thing. Even subsidising Christianity in schools and overseas missions. It was after all a purely Christian venture. People would say the religious types could always keep going one way or another. But setting up an *orphanage* through prayer? That would really be in everyone's face. If it failed then children would be seen being turfed back out onto the streets. Everyone in Bristol would know about it. The scoffers would gather, delighted, and Muller's ministry and lifestyle would implode. A PR disaster with God the butt of it. He needed to give it a lot of prayer and thought. Well, more prayer, really. He often commented how much he distrusted his own bright ideas unless he had prayed at some length about them. He spent a lot of time talking to Henry Craik trying to analyse his own motives. Would he be doing this for the benefit of George Muller or Jesus Christ? He had to be sure.

He began to pray that any idea of the Orphan House be *taken away* if not of God. He then bent his mind to other matters, trying to exclude it himself. But it wouldn't go. On 2 December Henry and he talked again at length. Afterwards George decided to hold

OPPOSITE: HOMELESS BOY (PHOTOGRAPHED CA. 1860). ORPHANED STREET CHILDREN LIKE THESE PROMPTED MULLER'S CONCERN.

a public meeting the next week and share his thoughts. Midweek for no apparent reason he was particularly struck by his reading of Psalm 81 verse 10: 'Open your mouth wide and I will fill it.' It seemed directed at him with respect to the Orphan House. But he had not been praying at all that day about it. Energised by this he went down on his knees and asked rather sharply for 1) Premises for the orphans; 2) £1,000 in cash; and 3) Qualified people to take care of the children.

On the morning of the meeting a large wardrobe turned up, which he took to be for the orphans, though he had so far talked to few about the idea. Despite this he felt very despondent. Until, he says, that night, when he got up to speak. He felt a familiar 'peculiar assistance from God' which he recognised from preaching – and that matters were being taken out of his hands. At the meeting there was, specifically, no collection taken up nor, he says, did he make any appeal to emotion or sentiment. But at the end he was given 10s and a women 'offered herself for the work'. It had been a positive start.

The next morning a couple came to offer their services, effectively as house parents, to any orphanage that might be set up – and they donated all their household goods to help furnish it. In the evening a church member brought 'three dishes, twelve plates, one basin and one blanket'. Within hours £50 had been given and the next day 29 yards of print fabric (useful for clothing) appeared. Two days later another member, who had obviously been doing the rounds, brought 'a counterpane, flat iron stand, eight cups and saucers, a sugar basin, a milk jug, a tea cup, sixteen thimbles, five knives and forks, six dessert spoons, twelve tea spoons, four combs and two little graters'. From a friend came 'a flat iron and a cup and saucer' and at the same time '£100 from a sister'. This last was from a poorly-paid seamstress who had been very ill for much of her life but had recently been left a legacy. After both paying off her parents' debts and much prayer she had insisted on giving the last portion of it to Muller's project, despite repeated requests to keep it herself. But she was adamant.

She said quietly, 'The Lord Jesus has given His last drop of blood for me, should I not give Him this hundred pounds?' Muller capitulated and accepted the gift. The lady remained unwell and lived in hand to mouth poverty for the rest of her life (she died ten years later), but never once regretted her gift, nor other small gifts she felt able to give later, as the Orphan House project grew.

For grow it did. Muller records lists of gifts of plates, window dressings, hot-water jugs, beds, tables, chairs, cooking pots and much more, along with gifts of money large and small. Page after page outlines each detailed circumstance, often surprising, quite often not. And all without any appeal.

'Through a "sister", given 6s, also a lady sent £1 1s as a yearly subscription' (Muller encouraged this type of regular giving if a donor asked to do it). 'A sister sent £5. From "E.G." £1 5s, and from a brother 6d. This evening someone rang our house bell, when the door was opened no one was there but a kitchen fender and dish were found at the door, no doubt given for the Orphan House.'

The long list of entries of this sort all added up to a remarkable day on 11 April 1836 when he opened the doors of fully-furnished No 6 Wilson Street, Bristol, rented for one year, to a group of twenty-six female orphaned children aged seven to twelve. One of the first was a 'most unpromising girl' called Harriet Culliford. But there were no 'good character' entry requirements. They all came from the streets and workhouses. Nor were subscriptions required from sponsors or distant relatives as the few existing London orphanages for 'orphans of gentlefolk' required. It was open to all comers.

There had in fact only been one hitch which Muller, with typical intensity, had felt was a sin of his own omission and therefore needed a full evening of repentance and prayer to sort out. Mind you it was an important omission.

At the beginning of February, with about two months to go and everything falling into line, Muller recalls he had felt satisfied he had laid before God everything he could think of concerning the setting up of the Orphan House.

A little later he notes rather ruefully that he had forgotten to pray for applications from any children. There were none!

He had been sure requests would automatically come. Guardians, magistrates or beadles would surely apply. The application date had been widely announced (Muller encouraged general publicity, he felt it was all part of the 'good witness to God's mercies') and orphans were everywhere.

So what was the problem? Muller suddenly felt he had been guilty of usurping God's role in this part of setting up the orphanage. It was God's orphan home and God should have been applied to for the orphans. He hastened to his knees and asked 'Him heartily to send applications'. The next morning the first of many was received.

Within a few weeks of opening Muller sensed 'after repeated prayer' he ought to consider opening an Infants' Orphan House for 4- to 6-year-olds of both sexes and then, when he could, one for older boys too. The pressure on his faith mounted. Weekly they plunged from destitution to deliverance. Then daily. Countless are the entries 'today we have only 2d left', or '1s remains only' or 'a halfpenny', or 'we have nothing to buy bread with for the children's tea ... but we look to the Lord for His provision'. And it would come, somehow or other. Just in time. Bread would be shared between houses. A ring at the door would bring 6d. Another might bring £5 with the giver telling a story of being tormented all day until they came round to give it. The Mullers would inject some money from their own income (also, usually, daily received). Receipts for some of the girls' sewing work would help, or gifts of material or household items surplus to requirements could be sold. Jewellery or other luxury items handed in as gifts would be traded for cash. Muller persuaded suppliers of bread, milk and groceries to accept daily payment (they preferred weekly) so they would not be tempted to run up any debt. Every day he and Mary would pray, and more latterly the staff too, and every day, somehow, they managed to pay.

Illness struck him down in July, preventing him from walking. On top of this the Mullers' own financial circumstances became desperate: 'Today, Saturday, we have 3s left, just enough to pay for a fly to take me to and bring me back from Bethesda tomorrow, as I am unable to walk.' (£5 turned up two days later.) Throughout, George just went on thanking God; and he soon realised his illness gave him time to get on with a new project – writing a book: *A Narrative of the Lord's Dealings with George Muller.*

This volume and its successors would sound him and his mode of living (and of funding orphanages) around the world. It would bring him the recognition he sought, not for himself (he even flatly refused photographs and portraits until late middle age), but for the God he loved and wished to show powerfully existed. It was to be a massive bestseller.

On 28 November 1836 the Infants' Orphan House was opened at No 1 Wilson Street and on 15 June 1837 he notes he received £5, a donation which would make up the £1,000 he had asked God for eighteen months before. Characteristically he underlines the fact that he had still asked no one but God for any of it, that only faith had enabled God to honour it and, while on the subject, it seemed right to ask God for a whole lot more! He felt the Boys' House should open soon and so requested his heavenly Father for funds to find and furnish a house for *forty* boys!

THE FIRST WILSON
STREET ORPHAN
HOUSES

Five days later the king died and an eighteen-year-old princess in Kensington Palace was woken and, still in her night dress, was told that she was now the ruling monarch of a global empire on which the sun never set. Thus, sleepily, commenced an era which would ever bear her name: Victoria. But apart from acknowledging her solid German ancestry, George Muller was unlikely to have been very interested. He was pre-occupied with arrangements for the Boys' Orphan House. This eventually opened in November, also, remarkably, in Wilson Street. A change of plans had been forced on George when residents near the house he had engaged to rent, in another street, had petitioned against its intended 'charitable usage'. Prayers went up and God, it seemed, quickly found somewhere much closer and more convenient!

The launch of his *Narrative* also preoccupied him. Though all the proceeds were to go to the orphans and to SKI, he had become so worried that he had written it for his own and not God's glory 'a sort of trembling' had come over him. But, reflecting how long and hard he had searched his heart before setting pen to paper, he soon put this down to temptation. He quickly broke open the box of 500 copies to give one away so, he said, 'the step could not be retraced'. Now his book was out in the open and there was no going back.

It recorded his life of faith to date, and the 500 finally ran to many thousands. It had an extraordinary impact. The worldwide preaching tours of his later years were largely the result of this and similar volumes being read around the world, and the requests to visit and speak that came back to Bristol as a consequence.

He became ill again. The strain and pressure of running three orphanages, ninety staff and children, two churches (with Henry Craik, who now took on the lion's share of this work) and the Scripture Knowledge Institution which was supporting a number of schools completely by now, as well as overseas missionaries, probably caused simple exhaustion. At least that was Muller's own diagnosis. Called by him 'a weak head' he wisely, despite his iron will, took time away from Bristol. Some time before, when his head was still clear, he had noted that he needed 'more time for retirement' (recreation). But this had proved impossible and now he was reaping the consequences.

He knew he was a workaholic, and indeed had blessed God that he was, taking the proverb 'the devil finds work for idle hands' most seriously both for himself and on behalf of others. But he knew he could overdo it, too, and when he did, he noted a need for 'a change of air' (never a holiday!). Fortuitously, money was provided by a timely gift carefully marked 'for a change of air', so he and Mary dropped everything (he could not now work anyway and had missed preaching at Bethesda seven Sundays in a row). They took a break by the sea in Weston super Mare and the spring waters at Leamington Spa until he grew better. The rest cleared his head, and picking up a book on the life of George Whitfield renewed his spirit.

Travelling to Leamington from Weston they had paused at home in Bristol. Sick and unable himself to go to church, Muller had looked out of his bedroom window on Sunday morning. He saw passing in the street thirty-two orphan girls from No 6 Wilson Street on their way to church.

> When I saw these dear children in their clean dresses, and their comfortable warm cloaks and when I saw them walking orderly under the care of a sister to the chapel I felt grateful to God that I had been made the instrument of providing for them. I felt that to bring about such a sight was worth the labour not only of many days, but of many months or years. I felt that it answered all the arguments of some of my friends who say 'You do too much.'

Bruised and exhausted he may have been, and new to his trade, but the apprentice robber had just glimpsed some of the jewels he had stolen from the streets. And thanked God he had been there to do so.

George Muller's life of prayer

Perhaps surprisingly, Muller often spoke of himself as a 'businessman'. He liked practical, accountable theology! He kept a highly accurate record of all his income through gifts and the sale of items donated to him, and turned this over for examination every year as his record of answered prayer. Down to the last farthing ($^1/_4$d). One or two years matters were so tight that he delayed this annual meeting in case people who came saw the books and might have later accused him of using the opportunity to hint at the need for money.

He generally encouraged everyone to keep a 'record of their answers' to prayer – and not just for money. Predictably he recommended an accountant's 'double entry' style. Requests down the left-hand side of a notebook, along with a date for first prayer on the subject. Then on the right-hand side a note of the answer, when received, with a date. He comments that he was always surprised to note the speed of so many answers when recorded in this way. But some did certainly 'tarry' longer for the Lord's time.

It not only took considerable courage and resolve to 'enable God to give' but almost a willingness to participate in a game of reverent Russian roulette. So often were the Mullers (and SKI and the orphanages) down to their last few coppers with all home-grown vegetables eaten, the last coals used and even personal savings of staff members offered, before the Lord would come through with a timely gift. There was little or no predictability in it. Muller's only comment on this was that timing was always up to God. He was certain God *would* come through in the end, but exactly when, was up to God. And very often it was at the last minute.

He said that anyone could pray for things in the way he did – and learn to expect concrete answers to prayers. In his *Narrative of Some of the Lord's Dealings with George Muller Vol 2 1873* he was particularly inclusive about this, stressing that everyone was *not* called to do work in the way Muller was, but that in each calling there would be answers of a similar distinctive nature, provided faith and prayer were exercised.

For our own prayer life

• We should prayerfully set goals for our faith. Few of us may feel called to live as extreme a Christian life as Muller – though maybe more of us are called to adventurous service than we might want to admit – but if our lives are so carefully engineered as to avoid the need for faith then we should not be surprised if God seems distant, or if He resorts to unexpected illness or loss to get our attention.

• Many find a close-kept notebook record of dated requests and answers to prayer an indispensable way not only of listing things to pray for, but as a record of considerable encouragement. We all easily forget, and to see something listed as 'prayed for' and then ticked off, is a concrete reminder. As Muller said, 'It is a clear testimonial to God's faithfulness.'

• Your circumstances are not mine. I might pray for something and receive it, you might pray for the same and not get it, or only after some time or more prayer. God is not being unfair. He is treating us as individuals, as part of His kingdom. I might not have your strength of faith, or I might be in need of more encouragement than you. You might need testing (as Muller would have put it!) or be required to learn more patience. Or it may be simply that the timing is not yet right due to a whole host of other things God needs to fit round providing your answer. Or the spiritual battle around you is so fierce that things are not getting through as they should, as the angel explained his own delay in Daniel 10:12.

> ... he continued, 'Do not be afraid, Daniel. Since the first day that you set your mind to gain understanding and to humble yourself before your God, your words were heard, and I have come in response to them. But the prince of the Persian kingdom [aka the devil or similar] resisted me twenty-one days. Then Michael, one of the chief princes [angel], came to help me, because I was detained there with

the king of Persia. Now I have come to explain to you what will happen to your people in the future, for the vision concerns a time yet to come.' (Daniel 10:12–14)

There is no true faith without holiness of heart and life ... [and] the true boldness of faith is known by its continually working by love. (August Francke, Christian Orphanage director 150 years before Muller)

CHAPTER NINE

Builder

30. Set in workroom – see the
boys' clothes are ready
the afternoon.

30 Walk with boys.

_____

sday:–
0 a.m. Quiet hour.
12. 15. Set in workroom &
workroom duties –
care for children
12.30. Set in workroom &
4.30 Set in workroom &
workroom duties –

_____

sday:–
11 Quiet hour.
12.30. Set in workroom –
duties

S ometime in the autumn of 1840 Muller engaged in an act of petty vandalism. He had been given a diamond ring 'with ten brilliants' by a lady as a gift for the orphans. But before he sold it he impishly scratched two words on the glass window of his room in Paul Street. The diamonds had suddenly seemed to him to represent all that God had given him for the support of the Wilson Street Orphan Houses (now numbering four) plus his preaching and pastoring of Bethesda and Gideon Chapels and the running of the Scriptural Knowledge Institute (which included the orphanages administratively while still performing its other educational activities). To Muller it was like having the riches of an ancient king of Israel. So, on the glass, in his round copperplate hand, he etched out 'Jehovah Jireh' one of his favourite Hebrew statements. For him a comment on the past, the present and, above all, his hope for the future.

'Which circumstance has often cheered my heart. When in deep poverty, my eyes have been cast upon JEHOVAH JIREH (ie The Lord will provide) while sitting in my room,' he confessed.

He would often have need of that comfort. In the 1830s and 40s income swung up and down. Matters became so tight in 1841 that Muller cancelled the Annual Report of Accounts meeting, rescheduling it for some time in the future. There was no spare money to hand. In December, the usual time to print the Report and hold the meeting, he felt that to announce 'want of means' would be tantamount to manipulating his audience. They might give in response to such an announcement and he wanted to show that only God was running the supply chain. A charge often levelled at George was that he made indirect appeals, or that his publicity was carefully timed to attract giving. It was something he was extremely sensitive about, so he always went out of his way to counter it. Cancelling the meeting was one way of doing this.

But by May 1842 further gifts had been received, enough to print the Report (copies of which were usually sold) and to be able to state at the meeting that funds were in hand. These meetings were always a time of general thanksgiving for gifts received over the past year (or seventeen months in this case) and, by definition, always showed that enough had been received; this time on 10 May £1,337 15s 3d. But the balance in hand for the future (to support 107 staff and orphans, ministries, etc) was £6 8s 10½d! By Monday 6 June there was nothing. The next entry reads: 'this morning I received from A.B. £50.'

The early 1840s were particularly hard George remembered. 'We had never been tried like this before,' he writes. Even staff members had needed to put their hands into their own pockets to help out. George seemed to accept this. Bed and board were always provided for his 'labourers' and they were paid a wage if circumstances admitted. If not, then money was stopped until matters eased. And if any came to individuals (such as a personal gift) they might offer it to help the orphans, though this was never demanded. But was this fair? Was this manipulation? Some would say so. We do not know what the staff themselves thought about this, but it does seem that all were conscious of the great experiment they were involved in. They worked and prayed together as a close-knit Christian team, and wanted to see their own faith in action. It was, it seems, part of the nature of faith to be tested, and never more so than in the matter of income. So they took the rough with the smooth along with their leader.

They worked and prayed together as a close-knit Christian team ...

But some giving George could not reconcile with his conscience. If he thought a gift was made on an ill-considered impulse, or could not be spared or, worse, was money that was owed elsewhere, he would challenge it. He would do this no matter how urgent the immediate need. The poor seamstress who had given £100 for the first orphanage was one such. Only after talking to her at length was George satisfied he could accept her money. A more difficult case was a gift of £100 from a lady at a time of very harsh need in the orphanages. George knew she had run up debts all over Bristol. He went to her and in a difficult conversation persuaded her she must take her gift back and use it to clear her debts. It was not the only time he had to do this, but it was one of the hardest, as the orphan funds that day were completely exhausted. Muller always saw such things as a test of his faith and his biblical morality. But it took some doing. Money for the orphans came from elsewhere the next day.

Times were tough personally. George's father had died in March 1840. He had managed to visit him in Heimersleben just before his final illness and they had had a good time. All was now forgiven, his father even admired what he was doing and was more than likely fascinated by the impressive accounting of the orphan funds which George outlined, even if he was unsure how his son came by the money. George had in fact paid off some of his father's debts in retirement and Johann was very grateful, understanding no more than that his son was, somehow, well provided for.

Muller was always sad that his father and brother, who had died the year before, never really took personal faith seriously, or made any clear Christian commitment of their own, though on this last visit George had found the words to try and explain personal belief to Johann directly, something he believed he had failed to do properly before. But there had been no response of understanding. And this lay heavily on Muller's soul.

Nevertheless they had parted with much affection, though almost certain they would not see each other again. George had prayed for his father much, without, he felt, achieving a spiritual breakthrough. But, with his usual magnificent resignation, he concludes, 'Shall not the Judge of all the earth do right?' God always knew best.

A key intention of the orphanage work, and one reason why it was conducted under the umbrella of the Scriptural Knowledge Institute, was that the children were to be taught the Bible and encouraged (but not forced) to make a clear Christian commitment; to find a personal faith of their own. Many did. Many did not. They were left to draw their own conclusions. Muller notes poignantly that while in Germany he had received a letter from Mary who mentioned that little Harriet Culliford had just died, still a teenager. (The average life expectancy for a manual labourer or servant girl in a city was, unbelievably, just *sixteen* at the time. And twenty-five in the countryside.) He remembered Harriet was 'one of the most unpromising children' but also noted 'she died as a true believer', continuing 'surely this pays for much trouble and much expense!'

But times were not always hard. If more funds came in than were immediately needed, the surplus was banked so as to earn good interest, or put aside for longer-term expenses. In October 1844, for example, part of a Bank Order for £70 enabled him to have one Orphan House 'painted inside and coloured down, which is much needed'. A convenient gift of £100 in February 1848 enabled Muller to 'get a new suit of clothes for all the boys, and give some money to the sisters who labour in the Orphan Houses'.

But by then George's mind was on more than the provision of clothes or food for his young charges. He was looking forward to a completely new, purpose-built orphanage.

Matters had come to a head with a letter from a representative of the residents of Wilson Street dated 30 October 1845. While courteous, the note had said that the large numbers of children were becoming an intrusion. The noise they caused at play was now continuous, as playtime had to be staggered through the day for each group of children, there being only one playground. Then there were the drains. Wilson Street drains had been dug for a normal residential street and the 150 (by now) extra little people living in it caused blockages. Muller had to agree the complainants had a point. He prayed about it and began to feel that there were a number of other problems with Wilson Street too. The single play area was one, but there were no gardens to cultivate either, something he felt it good for boys to do, as it required muscular work out of doors in the fresh air. At present all the boys could learn, practically, was darning and knitting with the girls. In fact fresh 'bracing' air would be good for all the children. There was also a lengthening waiting list for admission. Muller wanted to double the number. He wanted 300.

But he had looked the length and breadth of Bristol for something suitable to rent and could find nothing. Relentlessly, he began to feel driven towards the unthinkable idea of *building a new orphanage*. Unthinkable perhaps because it would require a staggering sum (£10,000 was his first estimate), but probably more because to him the sense of being a passing 'Christian pilgrim' on earth was lost if he made an investment in buildings and property. In principle he felt he should always rent. As ever Muller was getting to practise through principle, and he wanted the principle to be wholly biblical. After all he could not reasonably expect God

OPPOSITE:
MULLER AT
PRAYER
(CTA FILM)

(and that's who he was going to ask) to fund anything out of line with Scripture.

He wrestled with it, drawing up a list of pros and cons in his diary, as he did every time he had to face such a decision. In the end he concluded that building an orphanage for a Christian purpose was no different to erecting a new church building. It was all to be held in trust for God's kingdom anyway. And what a wonderful 'witness to His grace' that would be! He had come round to the argument that had led him to start the orphanages in the first place. And had they not been a witness? Certainly. His orphanage Annual Reports (no matter how late they were printed) and copies of his *A Narrative of the Lord's Dealings* ... were flying off the shelves all over the world. His motives would be very clear.

So it seemed good. And further, God might be asking him to do it. He shared his ideas with key church members at Bethesda. They too felt he was on track (mind you, they tended to think that about most things he did, the church had grown to about 600 by now!). He increasingly began to feel the weight of the words 'The Lord is near. Do not be anxious about anything, but in everything, by prayer and petition, with thanksgiving, present your requests to God,' a favourite passage from Philippians (4:6). So he, and no doubt Mary, the church, the Wilson Street 'labourers' and a host of others, started to pray.

Nothing happened. For over a month not a thing came in. Not even the smallest gift. But Muller was in a bullish mood. God was just waiting to show them the way forward with a grand gesture. Others were not so sure. A respected Brethren friend and minister in Barnstaple, Devon, Robert Chapman, was visiting Bristol and advised him to pray particularly about the plans of the place. 'God's plans' were what were wanted, he told George. George did not even have the money to consult an architect, let alone commission plans. He prayed on.

Then on 'the 36th day', trumpets Muller's diary, came the bombshell. 'On December 10th 1845 I received £1,000 towards the building of the Orphan House.' It was the largest single donation SKI had ever received. He had been right. But if anyone was looking for George's top hat to sail up into the winter sky they were to be disappointed. 'When I received it I was as calm, as quiet, as if I had only received 1s,' he wrote. Perhaps life to George was exciting and emotional enough on a daily basis anyway, but one can't help admiring, and perhaps feel a little daunted by, such superhuman, or maybe supernatural, self-control. His peace-in-the-Lord was certainly past the understanding of many. But, if visibly controlled, he always comments at the 'truly joyful' feelings he had at such evidence of God at work.

Three days later, his sister-in-law Lydia, returning to Bristol from London, said she had run across a professional architect. He had just read George's *Narrative* with fascination and had pressed her for all the information she could supply about George and his work. On being told of the new building project, he had immediately offered to draw up plans and to superintend the construction – all for nothing! Robert Chapman had not been far off the mark. George agreed. He wrote 'this is *sound* proof that God will help me in this matter'. Within the month he had received another £1,000 donation. He was as unexcited about this as the first. No fan of the theatre since his collapse in the foyer at Leipzig (he never went to one again), Muller was no fan of theatricality in life either.

> His peace-in-the-Lord was certainly past the understanding of many.

With money in the bank, George set out to find some land to build on. He wanted it within striking distance of the city, but elevated, light and airy for the children's health. Bracing as he called it. In February 1846 he found land for sale that was almost perfect, on Ashley Down, to the north of the city. He went straight round to the owner's house the next evening, only to find the man was still at work in his city office. Keen to close a deal, Muller strode across Bristol – to find the man had just left his office for home! Muller debated if he should now follow him back again, and called off the chase. Somehow he sensed God had work to do before the two met. He was not wrong. The next day an early call on the man found him in some agitation. He had woken at 3am and stayed awake until 5am. Lying there in the small hours he had found himself debating the land sale. After some tossing and turning he

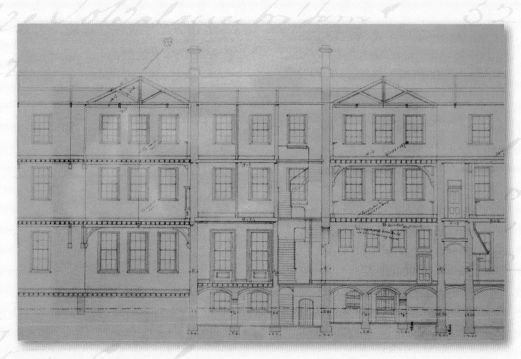

EXAMPLE OF ARCHITECT'S PLANS (PLAN SHOWN IS FOR NEW ORPHAN HOUSE NO 3)

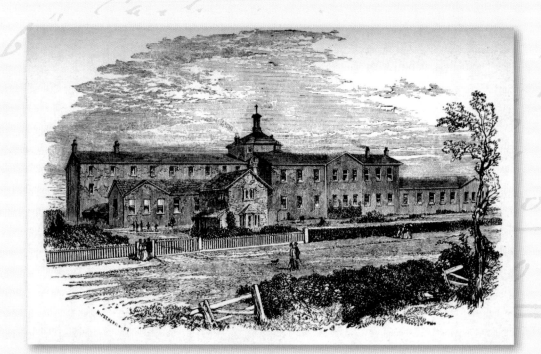

NEW ORPHAN HOUSE BUILDING

had resolved to drop the asking price by almost a half if Muller was after it for his orphanage site. George, quietly thanking God for His overnight negotiation, agreed the purchase there and then for seven acres of prime hilltop land, for £840 instead of £1,400.

By the end of the year gifts for the New Orphan House Building Fund topped £9,000 and counting.

Workers moved in on Ashley Down on 5 July and the foundation stone was laid on 19 August 1847, a year which saw the most severe economic recession of the century bite hard. There was a failure of both the grain and potato crop and thousands were left starving in Ireland. Prices doubled for rice, more than doubled for oats (porridge was the standard orphanage breakfast) and potatoes were priced completely off the table. Even bread cost half again. 'But,' said Muller, 'the children have lacked nothing.'

In the third week of June 1849, children and staff moved into their magnificent new 300-window Pennant stone Orphan House on Ashley Down. One window for every intended child. Here they could run, breathe, play – and garden! The London architect had been true to his word and had project-managed the whole thing. Costs, including furnishings, had come in a little short of £16,000. Gifts had topped that and there was more than £500 cash in hand. Muller wrote,

> After all the many and long-continued seasons of great trial of faith within these thirteen years and two months during which the orphans were in Wilson Street, the Lord dismisses us from thence in comparative abundance. His holy name be praised for it!

George Muller's life of prayer

Prayer-for-provision did not replace or preclude hard work – and self-help, such as selling donated valuables, knitted stockings or other needlework by the children, or enjoying home-grown kitchen-garden vegetables, though Muller objected in principle to long hours of work simply to bring in wages.

He once advised a labourer to labour less in order to have a proper devotional time in the morning and Bible reading time in the evening, and thus live a more godly life. To the man's complaint that shortening his working day (from sixteen to fourteen hours!) would lead to a very poor lifestyle for the man's family, Muller countered that God provided everything, even if worked for. So all that would happen would be that circumstances would fall out under God's hand and their needs would still be provided for. *As his family would find out if he died!*

Putting it mildly, this is a hard saying, but there is no doubt that Muller believed it, and lived by it 110 per cent. Such a statement, of course, implied a strong and submissive Christian faith on behalf of the man Muller was advising, an ability to 'trust beyond trust', almost in the manner of Job. Muller comments honestly that after this advice 'the man turned away still with doubt in his eyes'.

Muller saw God's provision in everything. He wasn't always waiting for an obviously supernatural miracle. If someone sold an old coat they no longer needed and gave the money for his orphans, that was God's provision. As was the doctor who refused payment for tending orphan children, or an unknown businessman who, unasked, donated a regular sum annually by cheque. To coin a phrase, 'all contributions gratefully received'. The only exceptions were when he knew that a gift did not belong to the giver, or that a giver was in debt and owed money elsewhere. In this case he would return the gift with an explanation. Bristol was quite a small community in the nineteenth century (about 250,000 pop.) and Muller was a long-standing resident who would have known quite a lot about local people and their affairs, though many gifts came from far afield and overseas. Gifts from India, Africa and Asia were not uncommon, his *Narratives* having been translated into many languages.

He did not view doing business as wrong or evil, just that he had not been called to work in that way. A Christian's faith, he said, should operate in all areas of a Christian's life. Nor did he criticise charities which undertook appeals and collections. He simply commented, rather dryly, that for a Christian charity the effort that went into fundraising might perhaps be better directed to prayer and discerning the will of God.

Speaking directly to Christian business men and women he comments that although the due process of trade was fine, a Christian should try to run his or her business in a distinctively godly way. If this was done faithfully and prayerfully then he or she could expect God's blessing on the trade. Naturally the keeping of good, honest accounts was one area, as was paying debts promptly and offering good service and sound, not shoddy, goods. This went without saying. But Muller was aware too of other, more subtle, areas to watch. He cautioned shop owners, for example, not to put someone outside in the street to grab customers, common practice in Victorian times, nor to dress their premises with over-rich furnishings and fittings, though all should be clean and neat (including the staff who, he says, should be properly washed and modestly dressed!). It was wrong too, he believed, to sell to a customer more than he or she wanted. If a woman walked into a Christian milliners looking for a hat then she should leave with one, not two! Staff were to be treated kindly, not expected to work over-long hours and be fairly paid.

Muller understood the importance of making income balance expenditure but maintained that good business was not driven by till receipts but by honesty, integrity and courtesy in all of its dealings, whether with customers, wholesalers, salesmen, servants or bankers. 'Then,' he said, 'you will have a Christian witness as God honours your business.' He tells many stories of Christian business men and women who followed these principles while also praying for their business. Many give large sums to Muller's orphanages as a result.

For our own prayer life

- No area of life – none – is outside God's interest or influence. Career, job or business, fixing the car, doing the ironing, making love, disciplining a child – all is life and Christ came to inhabit all of our life, if we let Him, by His Spirit. 'I have come that they may have life, and have it to the full' (John 10:10). Jesus' favourite title for Himself was 'Son of Man'. We will find if we begin to pray about our tough business or our all-consuming hobby or our difficult neighbours, interesting ideas occur (not all of them quite what we might want to hear – though some of them are more interesting and exciting than we might dare to think). God knows how a full human life should be led. He wrote the manual.

- Pray that work or recreation does not take away from our time with God. Jesus did not counsel us to take no concern over what we should wear or eat without good reason (Matthew 6:25). As Muller quoted endlessly, it is our 'treasure in heaven' that is going to matter to us in eternity.

- Hard work, though essential for achieving an aim, including a Christian aim, is not the same as prayer. Nor is it a substitute. Prayer (including thanks and praise) is a separate business and should be done separately. In this way work will be lifted and multiplied in its effect. In urgent situations, of course, working *whilst* praying is vital, but this should not be seen as the norm, and the activities are still separate. Concentrated prayer and concentrated work is virtually impossible simultaneously. Martin Luther famously noted that on days when he faced a full schedule he had to do a lot more prayer *before* he started work to ensure all went well!

CHAPTER TEN

Director

30. Sit in workroom - Let...
boys' clothes are ready...
the afternoon.

4.30 Walk with boys.

...day:—
10 & 30. Quiet hour.

10.15. Sit in workroom a...
workroom duties.
Care for children...

12.30. Sit in workroom a...

4.30 Sit in workroom a...
workroom duties. ...

...day:—
10 Quiet hour.

12.30. Sit in workroom.
duties

By December 1850 the New Orphan House was up to establishment with three hundred orphans and thirty-five staff. The space and freedom the new building brought was remarkable. A fresh spirit enthused the team, the old orphanages had been more restrictive than they had realised. The openness of Ashley Down was proving just the tonic Muller had predicted, though prayer was just as important there to keep things going as in Wilson Street. Nothing, even now, was guaranteed. But with a tangible building, something they could touch and see every day, they had all grown more confident in God. As one of the early Boys' House matrons once confirmed when a visitor had asked if their stock of funds was well invested: 'Oh yes, our funds are deposited in a bank that cannot break!' The visitor, impressed, had donated £5 on the spot. Muller's record of the matron's comments, and the outcome, is as predictable as are his italics: '… £5, which came in *when I had not a penny in hand!*' All supplies would continue to come in this way, as before, no matter how many large new orphanages might be built. George had an affectionate expression for the experience. He said that God was 'morning by morning inspecting the stores, that accordingly he may send help'. And noted, 'This way of living brings the Lord remarkably near.'

Muller also writes, rather endearingly, at the time: 'My labour is abundant, the separation from my wife and child great, on account of being the greater part of the day at the New Orphan House, sometimes also by night.' He missed Mary and her great support through the day. And missed seeing his daughter, now aged eighteen, but always his little girl. The new building, with twice the number of orphans, had made him a very busy man. But he adds, almost as an afterthought, 'It has passed through my mind to build *another* Orphan House, large enough for 700 orphans!' Mary's comments at this are not recorded.

But more prayers were offered and another list of pros and cons compiled, leading to a new conviction that it should be so. Another building fund was opened and off the merry circus went all over again. In fact a 700-bed building was soon seen to be too large and so plans turned to constructing two smaller ones to be called Nos 2 and 3 New Orphan Houses. Gifts began to come in almost immediately but there were many high and low points over

NEW ORPHAN HOUSE NO 2

LYDIA, MULLER'S
DAUGHTER

the next five years as Muller awaited the full sum. One high was
a remarkable gift of £8,100 in January 1853 from a consortium of
Christians; a significant low two years later when only just over
£400 had accrued to the fund in all of the nine months prior to
December 1854. Over 700 children were now on the waiting list.
But Muller felt he also had to wait. That was all he could do. But
he chafed. 'My heart longed indeed to begin to build,' he wrote.

Within a week he had been offered £5,700.

Work on No 2 New Orphan House started on 29 May 1855
and was completed and the building occupied by November 1857
(Muller was especially delighted to try out the 150 new gas burners
for internal lighting). Work for No 3 started on 11 July 1859, on new
land nearby which he had had a difficult time buying, 'but I was
assured God would help. And so it proved.' No 3 was completed
and occupied in March 1862. Muller had needed £35,000 to
complete the work to accommodate 1,150 orphans in all. He
received £3,335 9s 3d more – plus free window glass throughout.

But even by May 1861 he was contemplating, and praying for,
a larger work. He hated the inhuman workhouse system which
he knew introduced young children to vice and corruption 'on
account of the kind of inmates' and he had become aware too of
an imbalance between boys and girls in his own orphan intake.

ORPHAN GIRLS
WORKING IN THE
LAUNDRY

ORPHAN BOYS
DIGGING

Girls were always favoured as they were more vulnerable on the streets and more likely to 'be exposed to utter ruin if neglected'. In other words, they would be forced into prostitution or be left holding a baby as unmarried mothers, wholly unacceptable in Victorian times. At a practical level girls could also work in the orphanage until eighteen, helping with housekeeping and the younger orphans, before going into domestic service. Boys he would get apprenticeships for, but these would tend to start at age fourteen and, being always concerned for their souls, he had noticed that the age fourteen to eighteen was a crucial time for growth in spiritual understanding. He hated to lose his rescued waifs, even to an honest trade, before they had had a good chance to understand the precious gospel. Plus, increasingly, whole families of orphans were being offered to him and he could hardly take the girls without the boys. So he needed more room for boys.

New Orphan Houses Nos 4 and 5 were therefore planned for Ashley Down. Muller's fundraising methods were the same, only the figures were different. Again he had problems buying the additional land. His diary records long involved deals with the Bristol Water Works Company (by Act of Parliament they were building a reservoir on the Down) planning problems, compensations to owners for early occupancy and so on. George was no over-spiritual idealist. As well as praying he visited, networked, cajoled and exhorted to get a good deal. But it was the prayer, he said, that finally removed the obstacles. He never drove a hard bargain, only what all agreed was fair (the figures are minutely detailed) and in all of it Muller was keenly aware he was using 'the Lord's money'. The Lord's money from Hong Kong, from India, from France and from Germany, from Scotland, from Ireland, from Tobago, from Fiji, from all parts of the USA, from Wales, from everywhere. All individually recorded on page after page. But not all gifts were large. He often mentions small sums sent him with a letter intimating quiet personal sacrifice.

> January 4th. 10s 8d – with the following: 'this has been saved by little and little from my small trade. Many times, while this has been saved, my house has been without bread; but I would not take it; I looked upon it as the Lord's money. When in such a position, my soul has been much blessed in waiting for a manifestation of the Lord's goodness.'

Muller says this was a letter worth re-reading and 'I delight in recording it'.

Another entry read: 'November 14th. From a poor widow in London, who died suddenly, one shilling and a penny stamp, being the only money she possessed.' A note to Muller written before she died read: 'I regret exceedingly not having it in my power to send a larger sum; but I feel quite assured that my Divine Master, as well as yourself, will not despise the day of small things.'

> June 19th. Received £1 from a former orphan. And the letter: 'Dear and honoured Sir, Most probably my name and person will be equally strange to you, but not so yours to me, for when my parents were taken from me your home received and maintained and protected me ... I am now able to maintain myself and am doing so as a governess ... from my first earnings I wish to offer something towards the Funds of the Home which sheltered me when I had no other.'

Muller's comment on these and so many others like them in his records is written with complete conviction: 'they were laying up treasure in heaven'.

On 22 January 1866 George also had to confide to his diary the loss of a man whose lifetime of personal sacrifice had meant more to him than almost any other. He wrote: 'This evening, about half past eleven, my beloved fellow labourer and intimate friend for thirty six years, Mr Henry Craik, fell asleep, after an illness of seven months.' His co-pastor at Bethesda and Gideon Chapels, the companion of his youth in Teignmouth when the exciting experiments of prayer and provision were being tried out, the man whose preaching he admired well above his own, was suddenly gone. He was the same age as George. In retrospect George felt able to comment that God had upheld him at the time. But his daily diary reads more heavily: 'January 30th. The earthly remains of my beloved friend, Mr Craik, were committed to the grave this day; but I am ill at home, and became much worse this evening.' He adds a later postscript. 'For about three months afterwards I was more or less in a feeble state of health.'

George was a man of great faith, but still just a man. He missed his good friend, his brother of all Christian brothers, very dearly.

But important decisions were pending. The running costs of the first new orphanage (now called No 1 New Orphan House) had been £6,000 a year and that had increased to £15,000 with three built. Muller estimated that two more homes would make it £20,000 overall. All to be prayed in. On top of that he had been quoted £41,147 to build Nos 4 and 5. Could he do it? By May 1866 pretty much all of that had come in. But not quite all. He was £7,000 short.

Suddenly the cynics and the doubters seemed to change their tune. No matter about a few thousand, it was a worthy cause, surely it would all come in very soon? He was pressed to sign the building contract 'in faith'. It was a very good deal. A very good price. He refused. He would not even anticipate going into debt. If God had not provided then Muller wasn't about to presume.

He signed only for No 4, to make a start, well aware that the quote had been for building the two houses together, a much cheaper option. He asked if, for seven months until 1 January 1867,

NEW ORPHAN
HOUSE NO 4

NEW ORPHAN HOUSE NO 5

NEW ORPHAN
HOUSE NO 3

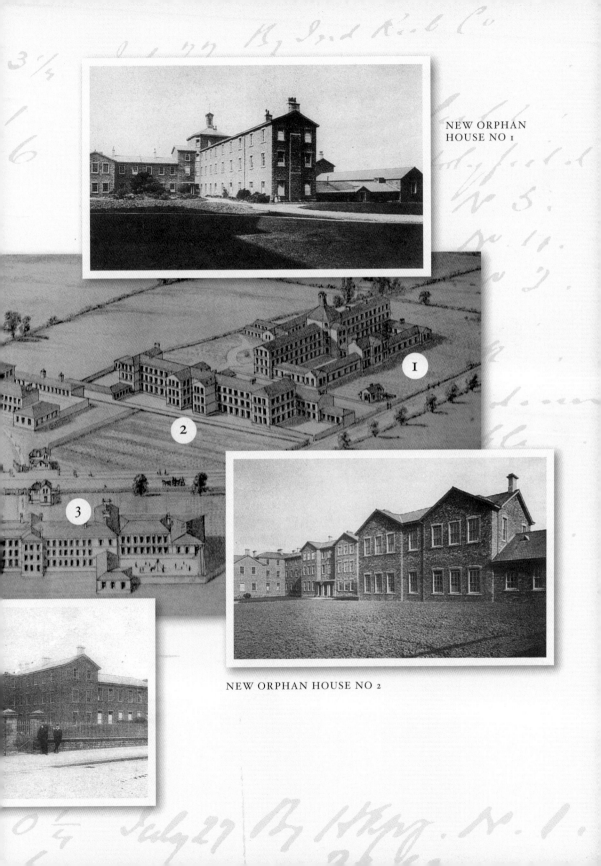

NEW ORPHAN
HOUSE NO 1

NEW ORPHAN HOUSE NO 2

the quote could be held for No 5 as an added project. The builder agreed.

On 31 December 1866, with well-concealed delight, Muller recorded: 'A little more than £7,000 had come in so I was able to accept and sign the contract for No 5.'

Once more it had come right down to the wire. Work started two weeks later and No 5 was completed in exactly three years in January 1870. No 4 came a year before it in November 1868. And once again all the window glass had been a gift. Muller notes 'and the greatness of this gift will be seen – there are above 700 large windows in the two houses!'

George now had ample room for his boys.

MULLER'S STUDY

George Muller's life of prayer

As we have seen, Muller did not just pray to bring in money. He believed that prayer changed all sorts of things and moved all sorts of people, not just Christians, often in strange and subtle ways. The story is told of a particular problem with a leaking heating boiler at the centre of No 1 House's central heating system at the onset of winter 1857. Calling the contractors occasioned much scratching of heads and it was decided major surgery was called for and the brick surround of the system would have to be demolished and re-built – a matter of a week's work. And all in mid December. Muller said he was prepared to spend whatever was needed to keep the children warm during the time the boiler was down, but in the end using gas fires or portable coal Arnott stoves was rejected as impracticable in such a building.

So in the end Muller prayed for two things:

1. That the boilermakers and bricklayers would have a 'mind to work' so the job would be finished more quickly. Muller was here taking a biblical note from Nehemiah who re-built the wall of Jerusalem in fifty-two days as the men had a 'will to work' (Nehemiah 6:15).
2. That the weather would remain unseasonably warm so that the children would not suffer from the cold.

In the event, on the day the repairs were started a cold northerly changed to a warm southerly and no heating was needed throughout the house. On the evening of the first day the workmen decided voluntarily that the best option was to work right through the night to keep up the momentum of work. The boiler was therefore repaired and re-bricked in two days flat!

Muller thanked God for this answer to prayer.

For our own prayer life

- We cannot presume on God, nor ask the ridiculous. Muller did not pray for the boiler to fix itself (though one can imagine an extreme situation, or an emergency, when even this kind of prayer might be temporarily valid). He knew it needed fixing, urgently. So he set about the task in both a practical and prayerful way. No doubt as his conventional options fell away he felt more and more that some special input might be needed. Having done his best he left the rest of the arrangements to God whilst feeling he should pray as he did. We must not presume. It is always God's interests we must have at heart, not our own, but knowing all the while He loves us and always has our best interests at heart.

- God often arranges for things to go wrong to show what He can do. If things run smoothly they are unexceptional. What interests everyone is what goes wrong and how it got fixed. A car journey is just a bore. But if you have a tyre blow out, drive slowly past a vehicle fire and then get caught in a snow drift it becomes a tale worthy of *Pilgrim's Progress*, certainly in the re-telling; though at the time we are fretting and fuming. As all the best business management courses say: There is no such thing as a problem – just an opportunity! And for the Christian a prayer opportunity – and a good story.

- If the weather is part of your (godly) plans it is not inappropriate to pray for it. No doubt God may have many contending requests on some days, and many other factors to consider in dealing with a degraded and fallen natural world, but as the disciples said wonderingly of Jesus, 'Who is this? Even the wind and the waves obey him!' (Mark 4:41).

CHAPTER ELEVEN

Mentor

30. Sit in workroom - till
boys' clothes are ready
the afternoon.

4.30 Walk with boys.

——————————————

sday:—

10 a.m. Quiet hour.

12.15. Sit in workroom &
workroom duties.

12.30. Carve for children

4.30 Sit in workroom &
workroom duties.

——————————————

sday:—

10 Quiet hour.

12.30 Sit in workroom.
duties

For the orphans, life by Victorian standards was good in the homes, though regimented and restricted compared to a life on the streets. One orphan remembered how his heart sank as the metal gates clanged behind him when he first arrived on Ashley Down in 1872. He had been used to the cobbled alleyways and bright lights of London where, true, he had often starved and shivered, but where he could at least run free. Now he would have a numbered bed in a dormitory, food in a dauntingly large dining hall, frequent baths (like it or not), laundered uniform (three suits including a Sunday best), and be expected to study from books (having first learned to read). The house routine started at 6am and there were house rules and regulations, the masters used their canes and the matrons their strident voices. There was freedom to go outside only at playtime, or during organised sports, or for older boys when the gardens needed digging, or when running errands.

In effect the five houses were a massive 2,000-pupil boarding school. For most it was a wonderful trade. In a society that looked down on the poor and regarded them as lazy spongers, that almost blamed an orphan for being one, kindness, warmth, food and clothing were hard to come by. But for some, Ashley Down remained a benevolent prison. Muller prayed much over those rebels, boys and girls, who disrupted life at the homes. A few were expelled. One boy who was on the point of ejection, having been both a frequent runaway and identified as an in-house thief, went to Muller for the last time. George closed his eyes to pray and put his hand on the boy's head. The boy defiantly kept his open; only to look up and see tears running down his mentor's cheeks as he prayed. It was a turning point. He knew he had never been loved that much before, nor would he likely be again. He asked to stay on – and did well.

The houses were divided into boys' and girls' houses, with smaller children being taken care of by older. Very small children were universally cared for by older girls under the resident staff, the older boys worked in the gardens to cultivate vegetables for the many tables. Both sexes were required to undertake formal fitness exercises – with rank on rank lined up in the playground to stretch and bend to a master or matron's loud command. The

CERAMIC
SHOWING
THE TYPICAL
CLOTHING
WORN
BY THE
ORPHANS

GIRLS
PERFORMING
SWEDISH
EXERCISES

boys had required sport – mainly athletics like jumping, running and tug of war, but no organised football or pitch sports until after the turn of the century.

The girls enjoyed active playtimes with simple ball games, outdoor swings and monitored walks, issuing out of the iron gates two by two in long winding 'crocodiles', their neat plaid coats and straw bonnets having become a feature of the Bristol city scene, as had the neat peaked sailor cap, short blue jacket and 'Eton' collar of 'a Muller boy' running an errand across town.

Muller's conviction was that it was essential for young men to build up muscles with work in the fresh air which, considering the apprenticeships they would be sent to, was wise: saddler, drayman, boilermaker, farrier, tanner, cooper, miller, grocer, butcher, ship's mate and so on. All orphans left for a specific job or apprenticeship arranged for them by Muller and his staff, supplied with three sets of clothes, boots, a Bible, travel money and a small spending sum. One orphan recalls Muller's dismissal of him to the outside world.

> He placed a bible in my right hand and half a crown in my left saying if I held to the contents of my right I would always find something to hold in my left. He then asked me

to kneel and put his hand on my head. Having prayed for me he quoted Psalm 37:3 'Trust in the Lord and do good, so you shall dwell in the land and be fed.' To this blessing he added a sincere 'Goodbye!'

Clerkships and other work which required more formal education was an option, but not a general route out of a home. Girls were trained for domestic work, as servant girls and occasionally as shop workers. They would learn much of their skill in the orphanage, doing cleaning, laundry and needlework, very precise with intricate samplers to prove it, around the homes. All were educated to a basic standard, and as the Victorian era spun on, these standards were raised to equate with the best in general society. Muller's SKI work in schools across the country gave him ready access to teachers and teaching methods and the best were employed in the homes. A wide education – much more than the 'three Rs' (reading, 'riting and 'rithmetic!) was on offer, with geography and history, English grammar, some classics, and of course a good chunk of Scripture.

In the 1870s a kind of teacher training college was set up in No 4 (Boys) House. Some of the brighter boys who had become Christians, were designated as Pupil Teachers. They were to follow a five-year plan of training and then could be appointed within the orphanage first as assistants and then as full schoolmasters. Some did so (others left for other posts) effectively spending all their adult lives on Ashley Down. The same happened to girls who had trained to be matrons or governesses, several returned to work in the very homes they had grown up in. One of the features remarked on by those who knew the homes well was the low staff turnover. Even though from time to time wages were held up and belts needed tightening, the homes provided a positive, uplifting and worthwhile atmosphere to work in. One orphan remembers the staff being 'strict, but never harsh'. George ran a happy ship.

Someone unconvinced of this was the novelist and self-proclaimed champion of poor children – Charles Dickens. He had heard a common rumour (of the sort which George admitted always distressed him deeply) that the orphans were starving and living in workhouse conditions. He paid a visit to Ashley Down to see for himself. George simply called one of his staff and handed him his keys: 'Show Mr Dickens anything he wants to see,' he said. After a brief tour the writer returned to London more than a little mystified, but wholly satisfied.

The high points in the orphans' year were conveniently spread: Christmas, Easter, George's birthday (27 September) – notable for the issue of 'Muller cake', and the annual outing to Pur Down in the summer. Each was an occasion to be celebrated with a thanksgiving feast, and kitchen stores and gardens were scoured for the best fare available. The content might vary as income swung up and down, but no orphan remembers a poor Christmas. Indeed it was George's stated policy that no child was ever to know the financial pressure of his faithful way of acquiring funds. The staff might know, the children must not. So there was always a tree in each Orphan House, dressed by the staff and hung with presents, gifts from local businesses, one for each child. Singing hymns and songs was a routine part of the children's life at the homes, and choirs were formed of the best voices to lead Christmas worship with carols. It was as much of a family time as could be manufactured for those who had none.

At the other end of the year the feast on the summer outing to Pur Down, a nearby heathland, was taken as a picnic. The

TUG-OF-WAR (ABOVE)
AND INFIRMARY
IN NEW ORPHAN
HOUSE NO 3
(RIGHT)

GROUP OF OVER
1500 ORPHAN
BOYS AND GIRLS,
TAKEN IN 1905

children set off, in the usual crocodile, armed with sweets and biscuits for the short journey. After playing on Pur Down – and here all the children from the five houses could mix freely – there was a 'ploughman's lunch' of bread and cheese, followed by games and then a large tea spread of bread, butter and cake drawn from massive picnic hampers taken to the Down by horse carts. A major logistics exercise for 2,500 men, women and children! And George was usually there, father figure of the whole; shyly approached by some, he was a little austere, but with warm, rather boyish eyes that smilingly welcomed those brave enough to try.

Though 1870 was a year of triumph for George and his mature, but childlike faith (he was now sixty-five), it was a year of perhaps his greatest loss. By now Mary had become virtual, though unofficial, manager of the new Orphan Houses as George had increasingly concentrated on writing, preaching and replying to the hundreds of gift letters now received every month. It was a job she felt she was born to do. She kept the books and regulated daily expenses, made bulk purchases and oversaw admissions and much else, rushing from house to house and then back home by fly, working far too hard. George knew this and tried to stop her overworking. But since he was as guilty of this as she, his pleas fell on deaf ears. She was as committed as he was.

She told him, 'I think the Lord will allow me to see New Orphan Houses No 4 and No 5 furnished and opened [her role was to be central in this], and then I may go home.'

He hoped not. But a month after No 5 New Orphan House had opened she was diagnosed with rheumatic fever. She had been ill before but this was more serious. She seemed to rally through January but then relapsed. She died on 6 February 1870 in the afternoon, with her sister, daughter and George at her bedside. After the funeral George records that he was 'very unwell'. The rake of Halle had become an affectionate and deeply loving husband of forty years. They had been very happy. Yet, devastated as he was, his faith that God had done 'good' even in taking her from him held. As soon as he was better he preached a sermon entirely about their lives together. His text was from Psalm 119 verse 68: 'Thou art good, and doeth good.'

He made three points about himself, Mary and their life before God.

1. The Lord was good and did good *in giving her to me*.
2. He was good and did good *in so long leaving her to me*.
3. He was good and did good *in taking her from me*.

In an extended speech he outlined the great esteem in which he held Mary, her godliness, her wisdom and her strength, and it becomes clear that the five new houses, indeed the whole success of the orphan project from the start, was as much due to her as it was to George. He certainly thought so.

He concluded, recalling her last hours:

> When I heard the doctor's judgement ... though my heart was nigh to be broken, on account of the depth of my affection, I said to myself 'the Lord is good and doeth good', all will be according to His own blessed character. If He pleases to take my dearest wife it will be good, like Himself. I was satisfied with God.'

That was the sum of the man.

ORPHAN GIRLS
ON SWING

THE ANGEL
WHICH REDEEMED ME FROM ALL EVIL
BLESS THE LADS

ORPHAN BOYS
WITH BATONS

10 to 12.30. Sit in workroom. ... boys' clothes are ready for walking in the afternoon.

2.30 to 4.30 Walk with boys.

Wednesday:-
9 to 10 a.m. Quiet hour.
10 to 12.15. Sit in workroom and attend to workroom duties.
12.15 to 12.30. Carve for childrens' dinner.
2.30 to 4.30 Sit in workroom and attend to workroom duties. Half the girls present.

Thursday:-
9 to 10 Quiet hour.
10 to 12.30. Sit in workroom, and attend to workroom duties.
2.30 to 4.30. Sit in workroom and attend to workroom duties. Half the girls present

ABOVE:
PART OF MULLER'S
WEEKLY SCHEDULE

George Muller's life of prayer

In the intense emotion of the loss of Mary, George shows something easily forgotten in studying his life of prayer. His continual *gratitude* to God for everything in life. As with the death of his son he could not, he would not, criticise God for the loss of his beloved companion. On the contrary he was thankful for the length of life she had lived. Of course in faith he trusted she was 'with Jesus' which was where he wanted to be, and fully expected to be quite soon. It was heartbreaking but not the end, not by any means.

Muller's attitude of praise-in-prayer and thanksgiving-in-prayer (to put labels on) is something easily missed when looking at his life of prayer, not because it is not there, quite the reverse, but because it is the prayer-for-provision which captures our imagination and seems to be the toughest test for faith. In the same way Jesus dryly challenged the Pharisees when confronted by the disabled man lowered through the roof of the house: 'Which is easier: to say to the paralytic, "Your sins are forgiven" or to say, "Take up your bed and walk"?' Forgiving sins was much weightier in reality, but being an invisible operation was easy to counterfeit; healing in front of cynical witnesses was where the rubber really hit the road. Either the man would get up healed, or he wouldn't (Mark 2:9–11).

George's prayer life was bedded and grounded in a life of constant discussion and communication with God, of asking His opinion, checking out how matters stood, raising concerns and issues of all sorts, but this was always – *always* – in the context of praising and worshipping God for His goodness. And this in every circumstance, no matter how hard or tragic, how apparently frustrating to the work in hand, or seemingly destructive personally or to progress for the kingdom. To this thanks were always added. Every corner turned, every tiny gift, even at the last minute after months and months of relative poverty, was accepted with thanks. Not just thanks muttered under George's breath, but stated boldly and extravagantly day after day. From his diary:

> Today came in 10s after lunch. Thanks be to the great God
> of heaven!

> ... of this sum I put £40 to the Orphan Fund for present
> use. How good is the Lord! How precious His help!

And the exclamation marks are all Muller's.

His diaries can be opened at almost any page and you will find praise and thanks. In fact let me take one completely at random now, 19 November, 1852. Here he writes,

> ... I wished to lay out more on the circulation of the Holy
> Scriptures and Gospel Tracts, but I had only about £90
> altogether left for these various Objects when I received
> this £200. The Lord be praised for His help and may He
> recompense the donors!

A significant element of this gratitude was due to George's lifetime awareness of his status before God. He never forgot that he had messed up as a youth and therefore how gracious God had been in redeeming him through Jesus' sacrifice on the cross. He could see it was undeserved, very obviously, in black and white in his own life, and so he was that much more grateful for being pulled back, for being saved, as it were. It was a favourite theme. Ever after he was grateful to God the Father for reaching down, for His Son going to the cross, and for the Holy Spirit working in his heart first in Halle, when converted and, after pointing out how far he still had to go, even decades later. He never considered himself Mr Nice Guy, even after years of faithful service. He was always 'Muller the sinner' in his own eyes and, he was quite sure, in God's. He deserved nothing so his gratitude was great. But it should be clear too, if only from his life story, that he was not Herr Doormat either. He had a robust self-image; he was confident and courageous. God loved him. It was his sin God hated – and demanded daily repentance for.

For our own prayer life

- We should always try to pray with a sense of praise, worship and gratitude to God. Especially (and Muller often counsels this) when it is the very last thing we feel like doing. Some people like to deliberately make sure of this by never starting any time of prayer with a request, but always with a statement of praise, or praise and thanks. Muller tended to read a text of Scripture first and then thank God for it before moving on to requests, offering praise and thanks again at the end. The order is not important, but the worship and gratitude is.

- With the personal gifts and abilities we have all been given by God we may become successful at many things so it is important to remember that we are still not all we are cracked up to be! Either in our own eyes or the eyes of others. We all go on sinning and need to acknowledge that fact before God in prayer as part of our daily development of our relationship with Him. If we don't, we should not be surprised if it grows weaker. Don't 'quench the Holy Spirit' with dishonesty.

- It is very powerful to pray through the words of the prayer known to many as The Lord's Prayer, but with care and thought, not by rote or like some mantra as is so easily done. Pray with heart and passion, really emphasising the words. As Jesus intended, it outlines so much of the business of prayer including worship and repentance (and a request for daily provisions). It is in Matthew chapter 6 (and also Luke chapter 11).

  'This, then, is how you should pray: "Our Father in heaven, hallowed be your name, your kingdom come, your will be done on earth as it is in heaven. Give us today our daily bread. Forgive us our debts, as we also have forgiven our debtors. And lead us not into temptation, but deliver us from the evil one." For if you forgive men when they sin against you, your heavenly Father will also forgive you. But if you do not forgive men their sins, your Father will not forgive your sins.' (Matthew 6:9–15)

CHAPTER TWELVE

Statesman

30. Set in workroom — Let
boys' clothes are ready
the afternoon.

4.30 Walk with boys.

———

...sday.—
10 a.m. Quiet hour.
10.15. Set in workroom a
workroom duties.
12.30. baths for children
4.30 Set in workroom a
workroom duties. S

———

...sday.—
10 Quiet hour.
12.30 Set in workroom.
duties

In the way of the kingdom of God many things had been turned upside down for George down the years, but never more so than in the closing years of his life. 'Many who are first will be last, and many who are last will be first,' as his Master once said (Matthew 19:30).

George had grown up a narrow-spirited, selfish hedonist who loved money, travel, wine and women (we have no information as to song), who loved to be the cool centre of things, the self-proclaimed smart leader of the pack, deftly holding together a double standard of worldliness and religion. Then one day he'd met, to his shock and surprise, a real Person behind the gowns and gargoyles he had thought were fake, and had given his life to Him. It was:

> A day when I died. Utterly died. Died to George Muller, his opinions preferences, tastes and will – died to the world, its approval or censure – died to the approval or blame of even my brethren and friends – and since then I studied to show myself approved only unto God.

And give up himself and all his desires, he did. He was true to his new light. And so gradually, over a long time, and never on his terms, he was given back all he had wanted. He married a woman whom he would come to love with a fierce intimacy of purpose far deeper than the flickering lusts of his youth. He shrank from personal publicity to find that his calling as a preacher, writer and orphanage director threw him again and again into the limelight. He gave up his salary and any hope of an official church position, and then proceeded to collect more money and meet more influential people than most Victorian mill owners, ship owners, colonial governors or world leaders would ever do. His personal support from gifts was far more than he could ever spend, either on wine or anything else for that matter, even if he had so wished – and he chose to give large amounts away. And now at age seventy he began to travel.

In 1871 he had married again. Susannah Sangar was a governess from Clifton whom the Mullers had known for over twenty years and was most likely a church member at Bethesda. She was sixteen years his junior. Many said at the time that she had set her cap at George and that she just wanted celebrity status alongside her new husband, insisting her name appear with his on church and other documents. Others said that she did not care for the orphan work. But whatever the truth of this she would prove the perfect companion for him on his forthcoming travels, the impulse for which was the literally hundreds of invitations to preach that had come pouring in from around the world asking him to visit and recount 'how he did everything with prayer'.

By now he had partially handed over the running of the orphanages to a co-director on the basis that he might die soon and it would be better to have a younger man trained up and ready to go. Muller was preparing to cast his cloak like Elijah, and James Wright was the perfect choice as Elisha, steady, faithful, prayerful – and good at accounts. Not long after agreeing to his appointment, his wife had died, so, eighteen months later, now virtually part of the Muller household, James asked to marry Lydia, George's daughter, aged thirty-nine. Wright was forty-five. Lydia was unsure. She had taken over much of her mother's role in the orphan houses and in supporting her father so she had not expected to marry. But George was delighted for her and

JAMES WRIGHT

this had in fact precipitated his own second marriage. So, with a younger management team in place, now he could travel. He dug out some invitations.

George and Susannah started modestly enough in the spring of 1875. George had increasingly felt that it was time to share more widely his insights on prayer and faith, and Charles Spurgeon, the noted English preacher, asked him to come to London to do so. Many came to The Metropolitan Tabernacle to see this German social pioneer whose work had pricked English consciences to care for the desperate plight of city 'orphans, waifs and strays'. Dr Barnados, Shaftesbury Homes, The Church of England Children's Society were now all organisations that were forming or had just been formed in the wake of Muller's Bristol homes. It was a packed house. George read from the Bible and delivered a text-based message, but what held everyone spellbound were the illustrations straight from the coal face. This was no theory. He had done it. He could refer to children and streets by name, to circumstances, to needs, with an immediacy they had not heard before. And he had done it, it seemed, in God's special way. The way of the Bible each one of them held. He spoke of his waiting, his holding on for funds until the last minute, day after day. Hours of rising early (he was a great fan of this) and of daily, persistent prayer for months and years on end. He enumerated the massive sums involved in the building work, the tests of faith that were still required. It was living faith. And his audience knew it.

And they did so round the world, attending his preaching in their thousands wherever he went. And he and Susannah went just about everywhere. In 1876, following two tours of the UK they went to Europe, crossing France and Germany (now at last a nation, pulled together by Bismarck, though with a Prussian military style that would cast a bitter cloud over the coming century). They headed for Switzerland and the Rigi. There was a lake steamer from Lucerne and a cog railway to the summit. George gazed out on a sight that he had not seen for fifty-one years. And the vista still moved him, but now he acknowledged God as the master artist of the magnificent scene. En route back home they dropped in on old Professor Tholuck, George's missionary mentor, now in his nineties (and responsible for enthusing and sending many German missionaries overseas). They talked long into the night. A lot of water had flowed under the bridges over the Saale.

SUSANNAH MULLER (NEE SANGAR), MULLER'S SECOND WIFE

Their first tour of the USA and Canada followed. They were feted everywhere and not only by the Christian community, both black and white, to whom he preached extensively in English, German and occasionally French. But, as Susannah records in her diary (she is best with the travelogue, Muller with the preaching contacts), they were invited to the White House.

Nineteenth US President Rutherford B. Hayes received them and for half an hour fired keen questions at George about his ministry. Then he introduced the First Lady, Lucy Webb Hayes, a noted supporter of the Women's Christian Temperance Union, who gave them a personal tour of the White House ('a large old mansion' adds Susannah for the benefit of readers who might not know!). 'Lemonade Lucy' as she was known after banning alcohol from the official residence, was a keen Christian, and one of the most popular First Ladies ever. It is likely she felt just as honoured to meet George Muller as the Mullers did her and her presidential husband.

The Mullers were to return to the USA for three more extensive preaching tours in the following years ranging coast to coast from New York to San Francisco, with a six-day train crossing in order to get a ship to Australia! Susannah's abiding memory of America was a wild stagecoach ride into the Yosemite Valley, a tourist trip she rather regretted, and a magnificent display of yellow Californian poppies.

'Wider still and wider' might be the words from Elgar's *Land Of Hope and Glory* reflecting the nineteenth-century expansion of the British Empire, but it might just as well have applied to George and Susannah. Not content with Atlantic crossings they went across the Pacific and Indian Oceans too. And this a couple who suffered sea sickness! But they tended each other through that and other ailments – George taking care of her on a particularly high sea off Canada and she of him during preaching in Calcutta when a fever struck him down and nearly killed him. On that occasion Susannah smartly organised a retreat to the hills via Darjeeling where the cooler air both revived him and helped him sleep it off.

They visited Australia, Tasmania, New Zealand, Ceylon (Sri Lanka), India (twice) and Africa, interspersing this with a tour of the Middle East including Palestine under the Ottomans – strangely unmoving for Muller, even when he was in Jerusalem, though he prayed that missionaries might be found to 'labour among the Jews', echoing his very earliest calling. They then went to Russia, the guest of a Colonel Paschkoff, a deeply committed Christian who held evangelistic meetings 'for the poor' of up to 1,000 *in his own house*! But Muller notes: 'this dear brother in the Lord was followed everywhere' by the Tzar's secret police and was eventually banished for reading the Bible to 'a few Russian peasants'. But the

Russian peasants were stirring. It was only thirty years later that they took over as communists.

It was in India in January 1890, during a heavy round of preaching in the central city of Jubbulpore that he learned by telegram of the death of his only daughter, Lydia, age fifty-eight. George had not even known she was ill. The Mullers immediately took train and ship for Bristol, to find the usual excited Ashley Down welcome at their return, from rows of smiling orphans, muted by the tragedy. But, acknowledged Muller, 'the whole work was going on so well under Mr Wright'. His daughter had been married to James for nineteen years. George's references to the loss of his 'dear daughter' are inevitably cloaked in the now familiar biblical assurances and, he assures us, so were those of his son-in-law who had felt it his duty to carry on regardless. He notes only that they comforted each other with one of his favourite readings: 'And we know that all things work together for good to them that love God, to them who are the called according to his purpose' (Romans 8:28, AV).

The Mullers travelled again, but this time just within Europe to Germany, Switzerland, Italy and Austria. The crowds continued to flock to his meetings as much to see in the flesh the remarkable man of faith as to hear his preaching. He repeatedly cautioned those who expected to 'pray for money' with the intention of storing it up for themselves. His was no quick-rich investment trick. 'But,' he would add dryly, with his gentle smile and Teutonic timing, 'the investment of your treasure in heaven' would be the wisest investment of all. As he had said a thousand times from a hundred pulpits around the world: 'Seek ye first the kingdom of God, and his righteousness; and all these things shall be added unto you' (Matthew 6:33, AV).

In early 1892 the couple landed in Naples, on the way home for the last time. They stayed until May, with George preaching often. It was an appropriate place to end their travels. Paul the apostle

> The crowds continued to flock to his meetings as much to see in the flesh the remarkable man of faith as to hear his preaching.

had landed in the Naples port suburb of Puteoli en route to Rome at the end of his missionary exploits. George was eighty-seven. In seventeen years he and Susannah had travelled 200,000 miles and visited forty-one countries, including many of the most distant from England on the globe. Like the apostle, they could record many trials and tribulations – no actual beatings or shipwrecks, though they had once come close. It had been an extraordinary preaching tour. George simply records thanks to God for the both of them being sustained so long in 'health and vigour'.

But it was not to last. In autumn 1893, 73-year-old Susannah became seriously ill, having been ailing for some time, and due to a fear of female nurses bred from personal treatment when younger, she would let no one but 89-year-old George take care of her. So he cleaned and bathed her, dressed her bed sores and helped her eat a little when she felt she could. He would attend her in the night when she called and left the house during the day only when urgent business needs pressed. James Wright still sought his personal advice and guidance (as he had done almost weekly by letter throughout the Mullers' travels). Good though his team was, the hand-to-mouth style of 'pray and pay' still benefited from the old pilot's hand on the tiller. And even now, with Susannah to care for night and day, George's diary never pauses with its total of weekly gifts.

Susannah died on 13 January 1894. For George it was a loss and a relief, for she had suffered considerably at the last. Alone again he moved out of 21 Paul Street for the last time into rooms in No 3 New Orphan House on his beloved Ashley Down, where he could continue to write and pray and be near the children, the staff and his son-in-law.

Ninety saw him in good health and spirits on the Down for 'Muller cake' with sultanas on his birthday and in Bethesda Chapel where he received a special presentation. He wrote that his mind at ninety was 'as clear and as capable of work as when I passed my examinations for the University in March 1825!'

OPPOSITE:
ONCE AGAIN
IN THE PULPIT
(CTA FILM)

In June 1897 he celebrated the Diamond Jubilee of the longest-reigning British monarch ever – Queen Victoria – whose uncle had still been on the throne when Muller had accepted the first orphans into Wilson Street. The Bristol City Jubilee Fund sent £50 for the

orphans to celebrate so it was arranged for all five houses to walk, in detachments, to 'Clifton Zoological Gardens' and be 'supplied with tea and an abundance of suitable provisions'. He preached a Jubilee sermon at Bethesda on the 23rd Psalm, emphasising less 'The LORD is my Shepherd, I shall not want', though he could testify, if any could, to that, but more 'I shall dwell in the house of the LORD for ever'. He was getting ready to go home.

During the summer of 1897 he was persuaded to leave Bristol for a few weeks to go to Devon. He insisted on visiting and preaching in Bishopsteignton and Teignmouth.

On 6 March 1898 he spoke at the meeting at Alma Road Chapel in Bristol, reading from the call of Isaiah (Isaiah 6) and the comments of John the apostle (John 12:37–41) on Isaiah. Notes made by those listening recall George's emphasis on Jesus Christ as the Lord, the link between the two texts. And as he came to the cry, as from Christ Himself, 'Who will go for us?' George asked the same question of all who listened, urging them to reply as he had: 'Here am I, send me!'

He returned to work at No 3 New Orphan House for the week, still praying, still counting receipts, still writing letters of thanks, still helping James Wright.

On the morning of Thursday 10 March George Muller was

FUNERAL PROCESSION (LEFT) AND MULLER'S TOMBSTONE IN ARNO'S VALE CEMETERY, BRISTOL (BELOW)

found lying beside his bed. He had died suddenly, reaching out for a glass of water in the night.

His funeral on 14 March was one of the most memorable Bristol has ever seen, with believer and unbeliever turning out in their tens of thousands to line street after street of the city for the three miles from Ashley Down to Bethesda Chapel for the funeral and then to Arno's Vale cemetery. Eighty carriages joined the procession. His grave was made with Mary and Susannah's.

Newspapers around the globe carried obituaries, but none perhaps more poetic, more accurate, or remarkable, than the United Kingdom *Daily Telegraph* of 11 March 1898:

> The far reaching effects of his labours can never be approximately gauged or estimated. He robbed the cruel streets of thousands of victims, the gaols of thousands of felons, the workhouses of thousands of helpless waifs. And he did it all – to use his own words – 'with the Sword of the Spirit'.

George Muller's life of prayer

Muller always stressed from the pulpit that successful prayer was allied to holiness. Both the holiness of the pray-ers themselves and the worthy nature of their motives in praying.

To a certain extent 'that is what he would say wouldn't he' may be thrown at this. He was bound to encourage anyone and everyone towards holiness. He was first and foremost a church pastor. But of course his view was that in truth no one was likely to be very holy anyway, no matter how hard they tried. 'All have sinned and fall short of the glory of God' he would quote from Romans 3:23 to any unbeliever, or even believer, within earshot. He was the first to condemn his own life, even after becoming a Christian, as 'the life of a miserable sinner worthy only of hell'. Like the apostle Paul, George knew just how far he really had to go to be holy. But to travel in the right direction was important. A process he knew as 'sanctification'.

He held that a pureness of heart and regular cleansing in 'communion with God' was essential to a believer. No one who 'walked in' what he called 'unconfessed sin' could expect to receive anything from God in answer to prayer. But he would concede that since God had undertaken to use him (a sinner) for His special purposes then God would probably be the best judge of how much blessing someone ought to receive in terms of answers. As long as, he stressed, prayers were always offered humbly 'in Jesus' name'.

He felt the same about motives. On his tours he often used the illustration of a man who prayed to be rich in order to be more comfortable, and was surprised funds did not come. This prayer, comments Muller, was selfish. It was for the man himself, not for the increase of God's kingdom or to assist the poor. God, he said, would not honour such a prayer. How pure Muller's own motives were can be judged from the high use of the funds supplied to him, though he was always content to be realistic and to take time off for a rest or a holiday if a gift came to him designated for that purpose. He worked very long hours and at times came close to exhaustion. Recognising this and taking a break was a wise husbanding of his own resources, not a reflection on mixed motives for praying money in.

As we have said before, perhaps Muller's ultimate key (apart from a personal relationship), to asking God to provide in prayer, was *believing it would happen*. The connection he had with God was such that he believed he could discover what to pray for (orphanage funds, etc) and persist in praying for these things. But to *believe he would get it* was the final, and possibly most difficult, element.

This is illustrated in one final story told by the Captain of the *SS Sardinian* a trans-Atlantic emigrant steamer of the Allan Line. Captain Joseph Dutton was known in the fleet as 'Holy Joe' due to his Christian witness and insistence on holding Sunday services on board ship during ocean passages. He always remembered his first encounter with George Muller's style of prayer.

It was on the Mullers' first trip to North America and George was concerned timing would be tight for his first Sunday preaching engagement in Quebec. Late in the voyage, fog shrouded the ship and Captain Dutton was forced to slow down and feel his way towards the Canadian coast. Muller went up to the navigating bridge and asked the Captain about their chances of making the landfall in time. He was told that unless the fog cleared, which was unlikely, these were zero. George commented that he was never late for such appointments if it could be avoided and so they ought to pray that the fog disappear. He climbed down to the chartroom with the Captain, went down on his knees, and prayed for the fog to disperse. Captain Dutton was about to follow his example when Muller put his hand up. 'Do not pray,' he instructed: 'First you *don't believe He will answer*; and second *I believe He already has!*'

Captain Dutton walked to the chartroom door to find the fog had gone and the coast was now in sight.

Interestingly, in his diary, Muller does not mention this episode which so struck Captain Dutton, who often told the story against himself in later years. Susannah only mentions fog delaying their arrival which, on lifting, had revealed land to be close. She notes that they berthed in Quebec late on Saturday 1 September 1877, in time for the Sunday service. Perhaps for them both, with good reason, such answers to prayer were routine.

For our own prayer life

- To reflect on holiness as Muller saw it, it is worth praying over (and around) the verse in Romans which Muller used – Romans 3:23

  > for all have sinned and fall short of the glory of God, and are justified freely by his grace through the redemption that came by Christ Jesus. God presented him as a sacrifice of atonement, through faith in his blood. (Romans 3:23–25)

- And to pray over these bedrock passages for Christian holiness from Romans 6 and 2 Corinthians 7:

  > But now that you have been set free from sin and have become slaves to God, the benefit you reap leads to holiness, and the result is eternal life. For the wages of sin is death, but the gift of God is eternal life in Christ Jesus our Lord. (Romans 6:22–23)

  > Since we have these promises, dear friends, let us purify ourselves from everything that contaminates body and spirit, perfecting holiness out of reverence for God. (2 Corinthians 7:1)

- And finally to pray that God gives us the faith, not to 'name and claim' in a flippant way, but to come before Him as children with real hope, knowing His love, and with confidence in our hearts to ask Him to do amazing things through us for His kingdom.

  AMEN!

For our own personal prayers – all we can do is try it.

ACKNOWLEDGEMENTS

First it has to be said that without the help of the modern George Muller Foundation in Bristol, direct descendant of the original, and still working to the same principles, this book could never have been written. Though no longer occupying the massive buildings which still stand on Ashley Down, the Foundation (www.Mullers.org) is busy in the same business today that George first established. So my special thanks must go to Wendy Clacker who regularly let me into the museum at Muller House and let me study in the library, and of course to Julian Marsh, the current Director.

I must also thank Crawford Telfer and Malcolm Turner from CTA, along with Glenn and Angelika Carlson, Wolf-Dieter and Antje Kretschmer and Annegret Schneider from ERF TV, Wetzlar, for help in Germany for the accompanying TV drama documentary and this book. Also Dr David and Rosemary Webster for many ideas and draft reviews, along with Lynette, my wife, and of course my generous, kind and efficient editor Sue Wavre (cheque's in the post) and the indefatigable Ed Pugh, visual mastermind and picture supremo, plus Lynette, Mick and Mike at CWR. Thanks also to Dr Stephan Holthaus from FTA in Geissen, Germany who gave up holiday time to see me and offered many insights into Muller the man, not to mention a map of Halle. And to Roger Steer, whom I have yet to meet, but whose established written work was my first encounter with George Muller.

If, despite all this help, there are some mistakes I must own to all of them and can only ask the reader's forgiveness.

Clive Langmead

National Distributors

UK: (and countries not listed below)
CWR, Waverley Abbey House, Waverley Lane, Farnham, Surrey GU9 8EP.
Tel: (01252) 784700 Outside UK (+44) 1252 784700

AUSTRALIA: CMC Australasia, PO Box 519, Belmont, Victoria 3216.
Tel: (03) 5241 3288 Fax: (03) 5241 3290

CANADA: Cook Communications Ministries, PO Box 98, 55 Woodslee Avenue, Paris, Ontario N3L 3E5.
Tel: 1800 263 2664

GHANA: Challenge Enterprises of Ghana, PO Box 5723, Accra.
Tel: (021) 222437/223249 Fax: (021) 226227

HONG KONG: Cross Communications Ltd, 1/F, 562A Nathan Road, Kowloon.
Tel: 2780 1188 Fax: 2770 6229

INDIA: Crystal Communications, 10-3-18/4/1, East Marredpalli, Secunderabad – 500026, Andhra Pradesh.
Tel/Fax: (040) 27737145

KENYA: Keswick Books and Gifts Ltd, PO Box 10242, Nairobi.
Tel: (02) 331692/226047 Fax: (02) 728557

MALAYSIA: Salvation Book Centre (M) Sdn Bhd, 23 Jalan SS 2/64, 47300 Petaling Jaya, Selangor.
Tel: (03) 78766411/78766797 Fax: (03) 78757066/78756360

NEW ZEALAND: CMC Australasia, PO Box 36015, Lower Hutt.
Tel: 0800 449 408 Fax: 0800 449 049

NIGERIA: FBFM, Helen Baugh House, 96 St Finbarr's College Road, Akoka, Lagos.
Tel: (01) 7747429/4700218/825775/827264

PHILIPPINES: OMF Literature Inc, 776 Boni Avenue, Mandaluyong City.
Tel: (02) 531 2183 Fax: (02) 531 1960

SINGAPORE: Armour Publishing Pte Ltd, Block 203A Henderson Road,
11–06 Henderson Industrial Park, Singapore 159546.
Tel: 6 276 9976 Fax: 6 276 7564

SOUTH AFRICA: Struik Christian Books, 80 MacKenzie Street, PO Box 1144, Cape Town 8000.
Tel: (021) 462 4360 Fax: (021) 461 3612

SRI LANKA: Christombu Publications (Pvt) Ltd, Bartlett House, 65 Braybrooke Place, Colombo 2.
Tel: (01) 433142/328909

TANZANIA: CLC Christian Book Centre, PO Box 1384, Mkwepu Street, Dar es Salaam.
Tel/Fax: (022) 2119439

USA: Cook Communications Ministries, PO Box 98, 55 Woodslee Avenue, Paris, Ontario N3L 3E5, Canada.
Tel: 1800 263 2664

ZIMBABWE: Word of Life Books (Pvt) Ltd, Christian Media Centre, 8 Aberdeen Road, Avondale,
PO Box A480 Avondale, Harare.
Tel: (04) 333355 or 091301188

For email addresses, visit the CWR website: www.cwr.org.uk

CWR is a registered charity – Number 294387

CWR is a limited company registered in England – Registration Number 1990308

Day and Residential Courses
Counselling Training
Leadership Development
Biblical Study Courses
Regional Seminars
Ministry to Women
Daily Devotionals
Books and Videos
Conference Centre

Trusted all Over the World

CWR HAS GAINED A WORLDWIDE reputation as a centre of excellence for Bible-based training and resources. From our headquarters at Waverley Abbey House, Farnham, England, we have been serving God's people for 40 years with a vision to help apply God's Word to everyday life and relationships. The daily devotional *Every Day with Jesus* is read by nearly a million readers an issue in more than 150 countries, and our unique courses in biblical studies and pastoral care are respected all over the world. Waverley Abbey House provides a conference centre in a unique setting.

For free brochures on our seminars and courses, conference facilities, or a catalogue of CWR resources, please contact us at the following address.
CWR, Waverley Abbey House, Waverley Lane, Farnham, Surrey GU9 8EP, UK

Telephone: **+44 (0)1252 784700**
Email: **mail@cwr.org.uk**
Website: **www.cwr.org.uk**

CRUSADE FOR WORLD REVIVAL
Applying God's Word to everyday life and relationships

Robber of the Cruel Streets Drama Documentary

A moving true story and a powerful demonstration of how prayer can change the world, *Robber of the Cruel Streets* depicts the story of George Muller. He raised huge sums of money solely through prayer and used it for his charitable work: housing over 120,000 of Bristol's orphans. In this way he 'robbed' them from the streets and gave them new opportunities. The work he started continues today.

The film is a CTA Production and stars Adam Stone as the young Muller, with Andy Harrison playing him as an old man. *Robber of the Cruel Streets* was filmed in various locations in England and Germany, including the George Muller Foundation Museum in Bristol.

DVD
Code: RCSDVD
£14.99 (plus p&p)

Video
Code: RCSDVD
£11.99 (plus p&p)

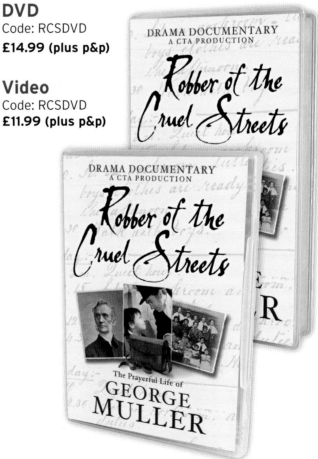